Sexual Harassment in the National Guard

THE FEAR IS REAL

Author
D Lindahl

A Mow-Time Publication

ISBN-13: 978-1482694758
ISBN-10: 1482694751

This book is dedicated to females who serve
our country in uniform. They give of themselves and
many lose themselves in the
unjust battle of sexual harassment.
Civilian females are not immune.

Out of 19,000 sexual assaults reported,
Only 3,000 cases are heard in court.
Most cases remain unreported.

*

This story is true.
Names and locations are withheld.

CONTENTS

PART I
Civil Service Career

*

CHAPTER 1
Take The Bull By the Horns

"So you don't like working here anymore?"

The twinkle in Kenny's eye overrode the sternness in his voice.

"No, really it's not like that! I love working in the construction field - the pay is unbeatable and you are a great supervisor! But construction is fickle. I have to think long-term. I need a steady job with insurance and retirement benefits so I can build a farm. I want to keep my daughter's horse in my own back yard and do right by her memory.

This is a state civil service job – like my dad had in Minnesota for the department of public safety – a career opportunity.

And I'll still have my lawn care business – I can mow yards for you after work and on weekends. "

I had filled out an online job application for the position Building Maintenance Worker with the Army National Guard. My interview at the Armory had gone very well.

The Armory commander and the S-4 sergeant reviewed my work history and took me on a tour of the facility.

After the tour, the Commander asked me. "Well, what do you think, can you do the job?"

The Armory was huge, I would have to override my fear of heights to access the rooftop HVAC units and I had never operated a floor buffer – could I do the job?

"No problem." I replied with confidence. "After all, when I began working for Kenny, I had never taken apart pre-hung doors to stain and varnish and then reassemble – but I learned and kept up with the carpenters. I had never worked with wood stain, but managed to mix a perfect match for the new trim installed in the refurbished Air Force houses. I can learn anything. Where there's a will there's a way. I looked the Commander in the eye and said, "I can do the job."

"Oh, Kenny, I hope I'm taking the right path." A persistent knot in the pit of my stomach seemed to carry forewarning – but I had accepted the job - Kenny gave me his blessing. I was going to work for the National Guard.

My first day on the job was Monday after drill weekend. Citizen Soldiers had come to the Armory that weekend to practice their soldiering skills.

The hallways were scuffed and dirty, glass doors were covered with fingerprints, the ladies' restroom was out of toilet paper and soap. I'd have to check the men's restroom situation later.

I went to my office, a long narrow room with a desk where I could put my purse and do paperwork. I hung my jacket on the chair and looked at the array of cleaning supplies. Unfamiliar chemicals were haphazardly shoved on shelves. Mops and brooms were propped along the wall and there was an unpleasant smell coming from the janitor's cart.

"Good morning." A male voice broke into my thoughts. I jumped and spun around. The Armory commander smiled and handed me a thick stack of paperwork.

"When you are done filling out the forms give them to the lieutenant in the S-1 office. He will be your direct supervisor - you will report to him."

The Commander looked around and apologized, "The building is in rough shape after our drill weekend, and you will be alone most of the day – we full-timers have a funeral detail – but, just take the bull by the horns and do the best you can."

I set the stack of papers on my desk. Where to begin! Everything needed doing at once. I put a package of paper towels on the janitor's cart, found a familiar bottle of Windex window cleaner and headed for the restrooms. I would have to figure out the mystery chemicals later.

As I was entering the ladies' restroom, a female soldier in an obvious hurry running down the hallway, stopped and said, "Hi! I'm the Charlie Company Readiness NCO! When we get done with this funeral I'll help you get a locker so you have a place to put your jacket and stuff in the ladies bunkroom. I'm so glad you are here!"

By noon my efforts were starting to make a difference in the building. The hallways were swept and restrooms clean and restocked. Trash and debris was off the floors and in the dumpster outside.

I sat down at my desk intending to fill out my intake paperwork. The federal tax information forms were familiar, but the state information forms asked for department and office numbers, questions I had no clue how to answer. I would have to wait and ask my supervisor.

Setting the confusing paperwork aside, I began sorting through the bottles chemicals on the long row of shelving in my office.

The sign beside my office door read "Facilities Maintenance." The room was a long narrow storage closet without windows. Floor machines were grouped together at the far end of the room. The desk stuck out like a sore thumb as though it had been shoved into the room as an afterthought. Sitting at my desk put me in the uncomfortable position of having my back to the door.

I began dragging floor machines toward the front of the office. After clearing a path, I began shoving the desk toward the back of the office. It made sense to keep equipment easily accessible for use and put the desk where my purse and records would be in an obvious personal zone – and I could sit facing the door and see who entered the room.

Next I began sorting chemicals. I was deeply into reading labels and groping cleaning supplies by their intended use when a male voice said, "Every dog rearranges his den to his liking."

The S-4 sergeant was standing at the door smiling.

"I see you've rearranged your office. The building is looking good. Are you finding everything okay?"

"Well, I am having trouble filling out the intake paperwork." I answered. "I'm not familiar with some of the terms – like what office and department am I with?"

He wrinkled his forehead and replied, "I'm not sure. We are all military and you are a civilian employee, so we have different paperwork. Oh, speaking of paperwork, tomorrow I will have you sign a hand receipt for all the equipment in here."

"A hand receipt?" I asked.

"Yes, you will be responsible for all the tools and equipment in the office. If you loan out a tool, you will sign it out and back in again. Military accountability you know."

"And, tomorrow the key control sergeant will issue your building keys to you. He's in the Headquarters Company office."

"Okay, sounds great." I replied. "Will my supervisor, the Lieutenant in the S-1 office, be here tomorrow? Perhaps he can help me fill out this paperwork."

I pointed to the stack of papers and booklets on my desk.

"I wouldn't count on it. We are all military and you civilians have different paperwork. Best thing to do is call your HR folks – they can help you."

I had no clue as to what or who my HR folks may be, but I had to drive right by the State Park on my way home. I stopped in and talked to the secretary. She was able to help me with everything but office symbols specific to the National Guard.

The next day I brought the completed forms to the S-1 office. My supervisor was not there, so I placed the stack of papers on his desk and left a note explaining that I had filled out the forms and was introducing myself to him.

Then I went to the Headquarters Company office. "Hi, I'm Donna, and I'm looking for the key control guy."

A stocky soldier with burly arms, very short hair, and a big smile stood up and said, "You found him, ma'am."

I was given several keys and instructed how to carry them. The master key to the building and the key to the lock on the roof access hatch in my office were considered entrance keys and were to be kept separate from other building keys like the key to my office (which for some reason was not in the master key system), toilet paper dispenser, and water room and miscellaneous keys.

My personal truck and home keys could be on the same key ring, but had to be easily separated from the building keys. I was told never to loan out the Armory keys. I could unlock a door for an authorized person, but my keys were never to leave my possession. Key-holders were subject to surprise inspections to be sure we were handling our key responsibility correctly.

The key control sergeant was hard core military, and a wealth of information about the building. I had so much to learn, I was glad I had found a brain to pick.

The next few days I spent memorizing offices, people, and creating routines. Monday, Wednesday and Friday were PT days for the military folks. Before work on those days, the soldiers ran and did physical training then came to the armory to shower change and be at their desks by 9 AM.

The Air Force sent a cleaning team to the armory twice a week to clean restrooms and buff hallways. Their work was provided in exchange for the Air Force using the armory for classes and events.

I began organizing chemicals and looking them up in the MSDS book which apparently was my job to keep updated and in order.

The floor buffing machines intimidated me and the metal ladder bolted to the wall leading to a roof hatch gave me cold chills. I hoped I wouldn't have to go up on top of the roof any time soon. But overall, I was excited and happy with my new job.

My office was beginning to take on my identity as I began hanging favorite photographs I had taken over the years. I had been a photojournalist and fire photographer in the days of Black and White photography.

My fourteen year old daughter's death brought on an unreasonable fear of the dark. I give up B&W darkroom work, switching to the construction field.

With the advent of digital photography I joyfully re-entered the shutterbug world. My computer became my darkroom to edit photos. Suddenly color was an option in photography and I began submitting sunrise photos to a television station. I carried my digital camera with me everywhere.

My Supervisor popped into my office on Wednesday to introduce himself and let me know that my intake paperwork had been sent to what he called the Puzzle Palace, the state National Guard Headquarters. He gave me a handful of timesheets and told me he had to send in my completed timesheets on the 15th and the 30th of each month.

He had an easy going friendly manner and a boyish smile that put me at ease.

"We are flex employees, so if you come in at 7am and take an hour lunch and two 15 minute rest breaks, you'd leave at 4pm. If you are a little later coming in to work, just leave a little later. Do you have any questions for me?"

I thought for a minute and then said, "I know the State Park employees receive training classes – I would like to take appropriate training to improve my skills and help me be more marketable or move up in state employment."

My Supervisor frowned slightly and shook his head. "I'm the military training officer, but I'm not familiar with the civilian side of the house."

He paused thoughtfully and then went on, "But you look into it, see what courses or classes there are for you, and let me know and I will see what we can do."

CHAPTER 2
The Nasty Guard

My new coworkers were interesting. There were eleven males and one female. The female soldier immediately took me under her wing. True to her word, she found an empty wall locker and we moved it into the female bunk room. There was no key, but the toilet paper dispenser key unlocked the door if I wiggled it just right. It wasn't really secure, but good enough to store extra clothes and toiletries in case I should need to take a shower.

"You will need to come to Monday morning meetings." my new friend chatted enthusiastically. "The guy who had your job before you always came to the meetings. You talk about the building and supplies you need at the meeting. Oh, and newcomers always bring doughnuts to their first meeting." She winked.

That first Monday Morning Meeting was intimidating even though I had come armed with doughnuts. We stood around the high glass covered table in the S-1 office. I listened to the good natured banter as we waited for the Armory commander to arrive and take charge of the meeting. He asked people to speak in order, following a progression that puzzled me.

After 20 years as an Army wife, I was familiar with military chain of command, but felt lost trying to figure out how the Armory was organized. There were only two officers, the Commander and my Supervisor. Each of the five companies was represented by a "Readiness NCO" who seemed to wear all the company's hats. The company commanders, as weekend warriors themselves, only showed up on drill weekends. The Readiness NCOs spent the month preparing their company for drill weekends.

The PAC office was the main office. The S-4 office was the head of the Armory supply system. S-1 seemed to deal with training and operations. And confusing to me was the commanders' offices – there were two commanders. The Armory commander had an office, and a higher ranking Commander occupied another office, one weekend a month. The weekend warrior commander seemed to be over the Armory commander.

I concentrated on trying to figure out what the people standing around the table did. If I were to do an excellent job of cleaning and repairing the Armory, knowing the responsibilities of my coworkers would help.

"Donna, we'd like to welcome you! Do you have anything you'd like to say?" The Armory commander asked as curious eyes turned toward me.

I hadn't realized that everyone around the table had taken their turn in sharing. My turn to speak came last in the chain, right after the National Guard Recruiter. I glanced at my notes feeling suddenly nervous.

"Hi, I'm Donna and as you probably know, I'm here to clean the building and repair stuff, so let me know if you need something fixed or cleaned. Um, I don't think I know enough to say much yet."

The S-4 sergeant smiled and said, "You will be coming to me for supplies – we are getting a new Armory Supply Sergeant, but she's not here yet, so just let me know what you need."

After other welcoming comments were made, the meeting was adjourned and I walked back to my office.

I noticed a male soldier walking down the hallway in front of me, giving the female Readiness NCO a backrub. I assumed they were dating – until I saw a wedding ring on the male soldier's finger.

"You look puzzled." A male voice startled me. I turned and saw the smiling face of the National Guard Recruiter.

"The structure here isn't what I was used to seeing as an Army wife." I quickly replied, hoping he hadn't seen me scrutinizing the very friendly backrub.

"The National Guard isn't the real military." He replied. "It is a state militia. Our Commander in Chief is the state Governor. If we are activated for duty in a war zone, then we answer to the President of the United States."

I shook my head trying to grasp what he was saying. "It will make sense eventually I guess, but for now I will just concentrate on the best way to do my job."

"Have you ever thought of joining the Guard?" he asked.

"I almost joined the Army." I replied. "But my husband was active duty, so I would have had to sign away our two kids so I could go to basic training. I wouldn't do that. By now I'm past the age cut-off."

He asked my age. When I told him he smiled and agreed that I indeed was past the age that even the National Guard felt it could recoup the expense of sending me to basic training.

" I'm too old to be a Citizen Soldier, so I'll just have to be the only 100% civilian here in this National Guard Armory." I said feeling pleased that I apparently didn't look my age.

Every morning I pushed my janitor's cart into each office and emptied wastebaskets. As the Readiness NCOs and the people in the administration offices got to know me better, they began to talk. I heard about wives, kids, pets, farm animals – whatever people felt like sharing. In the few minutes time I spent in each office, I began to get a picture of my coworkers lives, jobs and problems.

Drill weekends were a big deal. The focus of the Armory was all about drill – and it seemed there were two types of anticipation. There was a mountain of paperwork for the hundreds of weekend warriors who would show up for training. But there was an undercurrent of excitement. Drill weekends were seen as a time of fun away from spouses.

I began to recognize a "good old boy" system which sometimes went beyond job duties.

When the new female Supply Sergeant arrived, she immediately befriended me. She seemed to need someone to talk to and occasionally a shoulder to cry on. I heard all about her struggle in the National Guard to make rank without playing the game, without giving in to requests for sexual favors. She said that females in the guard were often expected to put out for the males if they wanted to make rank.

Rank-for-favors was an unfamiliar concept to me. I had worked for many years in the predominately male construction world and was used to being treated like one of the guys. I worked hard to be as good as or better than the guys.

The construction site was rough and talk was frequently crass, but I had always been accepted and respected for my skills. Period. Not once had it ever been suggested that a guy would "help me" in exchange for sexual favors.

Being a female soldier in the National Guard was apparently challenging in more ways than I realized.

Some issues quickly became clear to me. Drill weekends were partly training and partly party time. When I was on the Air Base during drill weekends I would stop by the Armory between lawn mowing jobs and watch.

Even though I was not on the clock, I often lent a hand or sat at my desk reading the building information books to see who would come in for a chat.

Weekend warriors or "citizen soldiers" stopped by my office looking for cleaning supplies or paper towels. The lower ranking soldiers politely addressed me as ma'am. Some soldiers voiced frustration and boredom – they expected more intense military training during drill. Others clearly were there for fun.

Once I walked into the ladies shower room where two of the female weekend warriors were looking at photos someone had taken at AT, the two weeks of Annual Training, the summer before. They were giggling, and quickly hid the photos. I pretended that I hadn't caught a glimpse of what looked like an orgy in the back of a pickup.

I later asked my new Supply Sergeant friend if she ever had seen drinking and sex during their two weeks of Annual Training.

Looking uncomfortable she lowered her eyes and said, "Things happen. But I don't hang out with people like that. I have a husband and I'm a good person. I do the right thing."

As I got to know her better, she talked about her frustration with her slow rank progression she experienced in the National Guard. Despite her self-description as a hard worker, she was overdue for promotion. There was a limit to the numbers in each rank bracket, and other soldiers with less time in grade had been promoted ahead of her. That seemed unfair.

Along with the emerging view of women as objects, I began seeing racial discrimination in the National Guard. The Delta Company Readiness NCOs was a black male. He had been in the Guard for a long time and despite his excellent recall of facts and regulations, he also lamented being passed over for promotions.

Sensitive to discrimination and equal opportunity, he gave me information to read and post on a bulletin board in my office. The posters were about sexual harassment, fair treatment, and the right of every soldier or civilian employee to take problems to the IG, the Inspector General.

It upset me to hear that my Supply Sergeant friend and the D Company Readiness NCO were experiencing discrimination. As time went on I saw evidence that supported their complaints. I wondered why they didn't do something to stand up for their rights.

Military command lasts for a limited time – approximately two years. One Monday morning, the Armory commander introduced to us his replacement as he was moving onward and upward. The new Armory commander seemed like a nice man, so I was unprepared for his chaotic reign.

One morning the new Commander asked me if I would like to join him as he walked his PT – he couldn't run due to a back problem and invited me to go for a walk. I politely declined saying that I'm on my feet all day and a long walk at the beginning of the day would take its toll on me.

After that, the Commander's attitude towards me changed. I was unaware of the invisible target on my back for having rejected him.

The new Commander tasked me with the additional job duty of creating and implementing an Armory recycling program. The Air Force had begun a huge environmental program called E-Camp and the Armory had to comply with the new standards.

I enjoyed my new environmental duties and had the Armory up and running with the new emphasis on recycling materials and proper handling of chemicals and dangerous waste. I was so busy with the new program in addition to my regular duties, I didn't notice that I was being watched way too closely.

One day the Commander pointed out that I was three minutes late coming to work. Startled and put on the defensive, I said, "Well at least I'm only three minutes late, not three hours late like my Supervisor often is." It was true – my Supervisor frequently came in late. Sometimes he didn't come in at all. I never knew when or if I would find him.

From that moment on, my Supervisor and I seemed to be at odds with each other. The Commander would give me information that would make me irritated with my Supervisor and vice versa. He would question me about my Supervisor's difficulty in accurately turning in my timesheets. My Supervisor and I were unknowingly being pitted against each other.

I began to see my Supervisor as a bungling fool who couldn't manage my timesheets and who had become a micro manager, making off-the-wall demands.

When the Commander would ask me how my Supervisor was doing, I told him truthfully how I felt, thinking that the Commander would be able to clear up the difficulty. Instead, the contention between us escalated. I felt personally attacked.

I've never been good at thinking on my feet – if something important needed to be said, I was more comfortable writing it out. I wrote my Supervisor a letter describing exactly how I felt when he undermined an aspect of the environment program I was implementing.

My Supervisor wrote an equally scathing and childish letter back. Embarrassed that I had stooped so low, I planned to apologize and try to regain a good working relationship – but I didn't get a chance.

The next day I was approached by my Supervisor, followed by the Commander and was taken on a "tour" of the Armory. My Supervisor was on a uncharacteristic mission to find fault with my work. He reached way above a hallway door frame, slid his finger across the surface and showed me that his finger was covered with dust. The Commander watched with a look of satisfaction on his face.

I was devastated! I took great pride in my work and enjoyed hearing compliments about my squeaky clean door glass, highly polished floors and gleaming restrooms. It never occurred to me to look for dust way up on top of the door jams.

Then the two men took me into the Commander's conference room and shut the door, which was in "lock" position. Once inside, I was presented with a negative "Performance Appraisal."

I quickly read the negative review, looked my Supervisor in the eye and said, "This is an illegal document."

"What do you mean illegal!" demanded my Supervisor.

"This appraisal is based on nothing. You can't do an Appraisal without basing it on a Performance Plan. You've never even given me a simple list of job duties and expectations, much less an actual Performance Plan.

In my search for training and classes I had stumbled onto the State's system of evaluating employees called the Performance Planning and Evaluation System. Since I had received no instructions or job duties, I had taken the bull by the horns and figured out on my own how to keep the Armory clean and in good working order – but I knew they had dropped the ball on my behalf.

My Supervisor's face began getting red. He squeezed his lips shut and searched for words to force me to sign the negative appraisal. The Commander seemed to relish the fact that my Supervisor was not successful in securing my signature.

"Also, it's wrong for you two men to have me alone in a locked room, scolding me, humiliating me and trying to force me to sign a bad appraisal."

The Commander laughed and then in a condescending voice mocked, "What do you think we are going to do to you?"

24

Fighting back tears, I stood up and headed for the door. "I am not signing that illegal appraisal, and I'm not going to sit in here and be bullied by two men."

In my office, I took several deep breaths and forced myself to calm down and think. I never expected to be treated in such a condescending manner. What to do? I supposedly had a "human resources" person - the posters on my office wall suggested the IG or a local counselor dealing with discrimination.

As it turned out, I didn't need to call anyone – I was informed that there would be a meeting on Friday in the Commander's conference room. I was given the phone number of a female sergeant who would help me prepare for the meeting.

I called the number and was immediately put at ease. I shared all my concerns with her. I told her that it seemed the National Guard preferred to "discredit the employee" instead of considering that the employee may have a valid point. She seemed supportive and understanding.

The meeting turned out to be a huge ordeal. The National Guard sent a female Colonel and a male civilian wearing a suit and tie, a lady who said she was my Human Resources person and the female sergeant who I had spoken with on the phone. The Commander and my Supervisor were also at the meeting.

I nervously read my list of concerns, which they called grievances. I expressed disappointment that the National Guard was not keeping the State's rules or even its own rules.

I had no Performance Plan, had received no orientation, did not have the required hearing test and physical upon being hired – and then instead of helping me do a better job I was humiliated by two men in a locked room.

I was treated as though I were military, but without the benefits of being military. I had even been scolded for coming to work too early. I had to drive a holding pattern around the block in the morning if I was too early in order to arrive exactly on the hour.

While I was at it I mentioned racial discrimination and the difficulties of female soldiers who were sometimes expected to do favors for career progression.

I even mentioned the violation of the federal food code when the Commander brought a road-kill deer to work and had soldiers butcher it in the Armory kitchen. (Commercial kitchens are never to have non- USDA inspected meat touch their counters or enter their freezers.) I also stated that the National Guard's own alcohol policy and the Air Force smoking policy were routinely violated.

I was treated in a courteous manner, probably because there were so many witnesses, but I didn't make any friends at that meeting.

My Human Resources person said that she knows what it is to be a civilian working for the National Guard and that we simply have to learn to be treated as though we too are military. She did tell the Commander to quit watching me like a hawk regarding my arrival time to work, and she gave me orders to use my chain-of-command.

The Colonel who was at the meeting instructed the Commander and my Supervisor to never be alone with me – I was always to have a witness present.

I was to receive orientation training, a hearing test, and as per state requirements, together with my Supervisor, we were to create a Performance Plan for me.

My faith in the system was restored. With naive idealism I looked forward to better days.

CHAPTER 3
Chain of Command

My original supervisor didn't have a chance to work with me on my Performance Plan. He was being sent away from the Armory for career training.

Before he left we had a heart to heart talk. He told me that he realized the Commander was pitting us against each other – and was doing the same to others in the armory. We apologized to each other.

It was true that there were other people at odds with another person – it was becoming apparent that the Commander was an obsessive clock-watcher and a starter and stirrer of conflicts between people.

My Supervisor arranged a meeting with the Battalion Commander, who was directly above the

Armory Commander in the chain-of-command. I was called into the meeting briefly and asked to share my experience and observations.

The Battalion Commander was a no-nonsense military man. He "promoted the problem" by moving the Armory commander to a position in Battalion Headquarters. The move appeared to be a career enhancing but in reality kept the Armory commander tucked away in an office where he wouldn't have to deal with people.

The S-4 Sergeant became my new supervisor and immediately began following the state's requirement for my Performance Plan.

He also explained that as my supervisor he was the person I should go to with any and all problems or concerns. It was his responsibility as my supervisor to see that my workplace needs were met.

I had unknowingly blundered all over the chain-of-command during my search for training/classes that I may be eligible to receive. I emailed heads of departments asking questions – apparently causing an uproar. People were threatened because I unknowingly "went to the top" looking for classes and answers.

The new Armory commander was a soft spoken Major with a twinkle in his eye and a firm grasp on reality. I could see my military coworkers begin to flourish. They knew what to expect and were being treated fairly. It was great to have both a good Commander and a good Supervisor, but it didn't last long. My Supervisor was promoted and moved up in the

National Guard system. His replacement, the new S-4 Sergeant, became my third supervisor.

My third supervisor was a police officer in civilian life. He was a man of few words who gave me interesting new tasks like inspecting fire extinguishers and the chemical storage areas. If he had a project for me to accomplish, he would describe the desired end result and say, "Make it happen."

My daily tasks of cleaning and floor buffing became easier and I had challenging tasks to look forward to accomplishing. Life was good in my workplace!

Apparently life wasn't good in my Supervisor's workplace however. For some reason the Armory commander didn't like my new supervisor. I was puzzled by the tension between the two. The concerted effort to force my new supervisor out was ultimately successful.

My female Supply Sergeant friend was offered the opportunity to move into the S-4 position which would make her my supervisor.

The Armory commander asked me my opinion on having a friend for a supervisor. I told him that I didn't see it as a problem – I was sure she would turn in my timesheets and get me paid. I was three years into my job and adept at cleaning, maintaining, troubleshooting and handling the recycling program. I no longer needed a supervisor to hold my hand and answer questions. I knew my job and did it well.

Taking the S-4 position was an excellent career move for my friend – she was nervous, but determined to succeed in the position and retire from the National Guard within a year.

I looked forward to a great working relationship with my fourth supervisor, my friend, and promised to help her write her retirement letter.

PART II
SEXUAL HARASSMENT

*

CHAPTER 4
Tricked

"Donna, I don't care if you're like 15 minutes late getting to work, I know you do a good job, and it's my job to help you do a good job. I'll take good care of you – I'll be your best supervisor ever."

Working under my friend's supervision was never boring. She asked me to help her with interesting tasks like planning the menus for the soldier's drill weekends – and I accompanied her to pick up the massive amount of food and helped her stock the kitchen on the Fridays before drill.

She also asked me to compose documents and letters for her and help her with her computer. She asked me to help her review line item numbers in the property book against printed lists. I enjoyed the diversity in job duties.

As horse owners, we talked about horses and hay frequently. Occasionally over long lunch hours she would take me out to her farm to see her horses, photograph them and give her my opinion on their care.

Every summer I was part of a hay baling team. I would store enough hay for my own horses and to sell over the winter months. In our hay talk – I told my Supervisor that I could let her help bale hay in exchange for hay or a discounted price on hay.

I emailed her photos that a hay team member took for my mother to show her how hay bales were stacked in a leased barn for storage. The photos showed me posed on top of a mountain of stacked bales pretending to hold a hay bale in one arm.

She never did take me up on the offer – I thought she simply didn't have time. I was a little disappointed as we worked together well. She and her husband would have been welcome hay team members.

I was puzzled by her request one day that I sit down in her office and list my tasks on a calendar, but doing so was not difficult · I knew my job inside and out – so I sat on her office couch weekly and outlined what I had accomplished. I didn't realize until months later that listing tasks on a calendar is what she thought was a "Performance Plan."

Her methods were different from others in the armory. She had changed the supply room system when she took the position, and the new supply sergeant was in the process of changing everything back to standard. It didn't occur to me that she may have a learning disability, and needed people like me who love reading and writing to assist her. I was simply happy to be busy and keep the Armory a clean and safe workplace.

When my Supervisor asked me to work overtime to help her get the Armory kitchen spit-shined and ready for an upcoming inspection I happily agreed. I could use the extra money from overtime pay – and I wanted to help her get great ratings on the inspection. Receiving commendations on the inspection would help her retirement process.

After only six months, the Armory commander announced that he was being moved to the Flight Facility. The mood and function of the Armory depended upon the skill of the Commanding Officer. I hoped we didn't get another Commander like the clock-watcher who had been moved out of the scene.

I was delighted to learn that my first supervisor, who had been promoted to Captain, was returning to take command of the Armory.

One Friday, while helping my Supervisor transfer food into the Armory kitchen refrigerators, the bottom of a huge box of lettuce began breaking. I made a wild grab at the box and felt a horrible stabbing in my left elbow. The box slipped from my hands and lettuce rolled everywhere. The young soldier who was helping us grabbed my arm to keep me from falling onto the floor with the lettuce.

By Monday my arm was still hurting. I went to my Supervisor and reported persistent pain to her. She had witnessed the event, so I thought she would know to fill out an accident report.

She told me to get the form, fill it out and she would sign it. I had to hunt for an accident form, and once again in so doing I trespassed into the realm of going beyond my chain of command. Human Resources again viewed me as a troublemaker.

I secured the proper form, filled it out, and gave it to my Supervisor to sign. She signed it and told me to make a doctor's appointment. When I tried, I was told that only my Supervisor could make the initial work comp appointment – but she had already gone home for the day.

I called CARO, the Central Accident Reporting Office to ask what to do. With CARO's help I did manage to secure an appointment for care and CARO folks suggested I find an attorney to help me with future appointments and paperwork.

AFSCME, a brand new state employee's union, advertised workman's compensation attorneys. I chose an attorney, became active with the employees union, and that too was considered a threat.

My elbow became a serious problem. I was placed on and off of light duty, given cortisone injections – but the painful condition called "tennis elbow" persisted. It was becoming difficult to do mop floors and run the floor buffers. I worked through the pain, but worried that my elbow was being damaged.

Shortly after my original supervisor took command, the Armory gained a new Operations Sergeant. As a Master Sergeant (MSGT), he was the highest ranking NCO in the Armory.

The MSGT was friendly and sometimes stopped by my office to chat or ask me to do tasks for him. While I reported directly to my Supervisor, anyone in the Armory could ask me to do something for them, like install a message board or hang pictures. I learned that the new MSGT had diabetes. My mom raised me as health nut. Vitamins and exercise were second nature to me.

Recognizing common ground, the MSGT talked about blood sugar control through food and supplements and exercise. If he were required to be on insulin it would make him non-combat ready – a career buster.

One day the MSGT stopped by my office to get some window cleaner. He noticed a photo I had posted on the Chemical Locker. Another female in the Armory had sent me the photo asking if I would print it out in color at home for her. When I did, I made a copy for myself.

The photo was an 8x10 of the back of man sporting a military haircut – looking over his shoulder with an American Flag draped across his back revealing a very muscular shoulder and back.

The MSGT said, "I see you have a picture of me on your locker."

I laughed. There was no comparison between the MSGT and the buff man in the photo.

From that time on, the MSGT occasionally would comment on "his" picture on my Chemical Locker. Then he began asking me when I was going to re-take the photo of him, to which I would reply, "Ya right." It was an obvious joke.

On the Friday before Labor Day weekend, the military Armory personnel were given the day off. As a civilian employee I wasn't allowed to take the day off – but I was glad to have the Armory free of people. I would be able to mop and burnish hallways and the drill floor with nobody in my way.

I camped out in the PAC office to be near the entry door, which I had unlocked so I could receive mail and UPS deliveries.

Restrooms were cleaned and I was heading to the drill floor with a dust mop when I heard a door being unlocked on the west end of the building by the dumpster.

I froze. Then saw that it was the MSGT. He was wearing his PT shorts and t-shirt. He walked down the hallway towards the PAC office and asked, "Where is everybody?"

I thought it odd that the chief NCO in the Armory didn't know about the military "down day" to extend the Labor Day weekend into a four-day vacation, but I explained it to him anyway.

"You've got your camera with you, now you can re-take that picture of me in the flag."

The last thing I felt like doing was posing a photo of him trying to look like the guy in the photo on my locker.

"Na, I've got the drill floor to burnish." I politely declined.

"Aw, come on – you've got your camera – I'll go find a flag and you can take my picture." He insisted.

"No, really, I need to get busy on the floor." I said, but he wouldn't take 'no' for an answer.

"Oh all right, go find a flag. I'll work on the drill floor." I said, thinking that he would go to the Commander's office where I had seen flags in boxes ready for funeral details.

I had dust mopped about 1/3 of the huge drill floor when I heard his voice, "Ok. I found a flag. I'm ready in the locker room. Get your camera."

I set the dust mop down marking my place and went to the PAC office. Then with camera in hand I went to the male locker room.

I walked into the locker room looking down at my camera settings. When I looked up I was shocked to see the MSGT standing totally nude facing me with a tiny paper American Flag covering his private parts.

He laughed as I gasped and said, "Take the picture."

I pushed the shutter. The camera clicked but the flash didn't go off.

"Again" he said as he raised the flag to his chest leaving his private parts exposed.

My hands were shaking so I could barely hold the camera. I pushed the shutter again with the distinct feeling that this had become an evidence photo.

I turned to leave and he said, "Wait. You undress and let me photograph you with my mind."

"No way in hell!" I replied. "I'm not going to jail!"

I ran back to the PAC office, feeling ill and trembling. I set my camera down on the desk beside my purse and slumped into a chair.

"What do I do now?" I wondered, shaken and afraid. My Supervisor was away with her family on a horseback camping trip – I couldn't call her. I was afraid to leave the PAC office where there were windows. I tried to calm down and collect my thoughts.

"You sure looked nervous." The MSGT's voice startled me as he walked into the office with a smile on his face,

"Let's see the pictures."

He picked up my camera and looked at the view pane on back.

"Guess I better get rid of these – don't want you putting them on the internet." He began pushing buttons and I could hear the floppy disk inside whirring.

I was surprised. I thought the floppy disk had to be put into a computer in order to edit or delete photos. I sat quietly, barely breathing.

After deleting the photos from my camera, he said, "This is bullshit that you have to work today. Go home."

In my supervisor's absence any of the military folks became my default supervisor – and he being the highest ranking NCO in the Armory, I figured he had double authority to send me home. I didn't need to be told twice. I beat feet out of there.

It was a long weekend in two ways for me I hadn't wanted to take photos of the MSGT in the first place – and then instead of replicating the photo on my locker by posing with a full sized American Flag, he had set me up to expose himself to me. I was alone and feeling that I had been tricked and violated.

Tuesday morning, as soon as my Supervisor arrived at her office, I followed her in and shut the door behind us. When I described what the MSGT had done, she looked like she wanted to cry.

"Why would he do that?" She asked.

"He's a sick puppy." Was the only answer I could think of.

"Do you have proof?"

Startled, I shook my head. "No. He deleted the photos right off my camera. I didn't know you could do that. I thought the floppy drive had to be edited in a computer." I replied.

"Well you need proof." She said resolutely.

I understood. I was presenting my Supervisor with a difficult problem by telling her the horrible thing that the MSGT, her own superior, had done to me. He played a crucial role in her successful retirement. She was between a rock and a very hard place.

I left her office feeling sorry for my Supervisor. She always talked about doing the right thing – I figured she would take care of the problem somehow.

As for me, I would never be tricked into taking a photo of the MSGT again!

CHAPTER 5
Harassed

Gradually I felt less upset and put the incident behind me. Several months later, I was pushing my noisy janitor's cart down the hallway to begin my trash pickup from offices – as I passed the doorway to the men's locker room, the MSGT suddenly stepped out of the shadows.

The unexpected motion caught my attention and I turned to look. He had pulled his gym shorts down and pointed his erect penis at me. I gasped and hurried to push my cart down the hall towards the offices and safety. As I ran away, I heard him laughing.

I bypassed offices and went directly to the S-4 office to find my Supervisor. She wasn't there. I parked my cart and went looking for her. She was in the female restroom.

When I described what had just happened she looked uncomfortable.

"Do you have proof?" She asked.

"Proof! No! I didn't even know he was there until he stepped out of the shadows waving his penis at me." I replied fighting back a feeling of nausea.

"Well, you need proof. I'm sorry."

Shaken and angry, I left the restroom and resumed my rounds. Several coworkers asked if I was okay.

"I'll be all right." I answered and then turned the conversation towards them and how their day was going. People liked sharing with me. Maybe because I didn't wear a military uniform, they felt particularly comfortable talking about their worries and their families.

I had a farm, knew how to run hay equipment, and handle livestock - coworkers with agriculture backgrounds enjoyed talking farm with me. Mothers talked about their children. Pet owners talked about their dogs or cats.

People shared their stories with me – perhaps because they sensed my genuine concern and interest. But when I was upset or had difficulty, I bottled it up inside. Ever since I was grade school kid, I couldn't talk about things that hurt or upset me.

I realized that had to get a grip on myself, by myself. It looked as though I'd have to start carrying my camera daily to catch the MSGT in case he flashed me again. I hoped to God I wouldn't have an opportunity to get the proof my Supervisor said was necessary.

Over the next few months the MSGT did flash me several times. He changed his location. I never knew where he would show up with his pants down but it was always when he was quite sure nobody else was nearby.

When exposed himself he would look down at his penis and talk about his flag. My camera was never on my janitor's cart when I needed it – though I was not sure I would have been able to take a photo. It was hard to control my fear as I ran away.

The MSGT seemed to delight in my panicked reaction to being flashed. He blocked my escape once and asked me if I liked his "flag" half staff or full mast. He was getting weirder and scarier.

There was usually a span of a month or more between flashing incidents. I was finding it difficult to sleep at night. When I did sleep I had a recurring dream about being unable to escape some unidentified danger. I would run, but the ground under me was like a conveyor belt. My feet would move, but I remained in the path of danger.

One morning I was just pushing my janitors cart out of my office door when the MSGT appeared and blocked my path.
He told me to go back into my office with him because he wanted to show me that his flag was flying.

"I can't do that." I said, feeling sick and scared. "Besides I don't have my camera."

While he undoubtedly was not aware of my Supervisor's mandate that I get proof, I babbled about not having my camera as I pushed my cart past him out into the hallway. I hurried to work in a populated part of the Armory, relieved that this time he hadn't flashed me.

After an hour I returned to my office, parked my cart and sat down at my desk. While bending over to get my purse out of the bottom drawer, I heard my office door click shut. The hair prickled on the back of my neck and I sat upright.

Still wearing gym shorts and a tee shirt, the MSGT pushed the lock button on the door handle and stood facing me. I was trapped in my long narrow windowless office.

"My flag is full mast." He commented with a smile and began walking towards me as he pulled his gym shorts down.

"Do you like my flag at half staff or full mast?"

Panic flooded me. I quickly stood up. Standing freed my feet to kick. I curled my fingers around a piece of wood on my desktop – a six inch piece I had sawed off the end of the Commander's flagpole enabling the flag to fit in his conference room. The hunk of wood wasn't much of a weapon, but better than nothing.

"I'm just a little guy," He said and started walking towards me.

My peripheral vision darkened – all I saw was the MSGT. When he reached my chemical locker he stopped and looked at the photo of the man with the flag draped across his back.

"I'm a little guy...with a big flag."

He turned sideways to me with his back to the chemical locker and began playing with his penis. I noticed a dark discoloration like a mole on his right

46

testicle. Then looking upward, he began rubbing his penis. Before he could make a move towards me he would have to lower his eyes and look my way. I stared at his face, watching for any sign of movement towards me.

I wanted to run out of my office, but if I tried to escape, I would place myself within his reach.

Desperately I tried to remember what women are supposed to do when faced with rape or sexual assault. There was something about not angering or upsetting the aggressor – and something about talking calmly.

Cautiously I asked, "What, does it work better if someone watches?"

Without answering he nodded his head and continued to rub his penis.

"That is so sick!" I thought to myself. Then the room started to spin – I realized I had been holding my breath. I forced myself to take a slow deep breath. I felt my nostrils flaring as I stared at his face.

Suddenly without a sound, he stopped and stared at my storage shelves. He stepped forward, grabbed a towel and began wiping his hands and private parts. Then as abruptly as he appeared he left, taking the towel with him.

I sat still, listening to be sure the MSGT was really gone. After a few minutes I walked quietly to the door and looked down the hallway. It was empty. Still clutching the sawed off piece of wood, I hurried across the drill floor, through the rotunda and to my Supervisor's office.

Busily working on a problem with her computer, she glanced up when she saw me.

"The MSGT..." I faltered, trying to compose myself. "He...."

As I told her what had just happened, she continued working on her computer.

"Keep talking, I'm listening." She said, avoiding looking at me as I spoke. Her face blanched when she heard about the MSGT having locked me in my office and then masturbating in front of me, but instead of consolation or reassurance, she again asked, "Do you have proof?"

Clearly my Supervisor did not want to hear what I had to tell her. She focused her attention on her computer problem apparently afraid to make waves in the Armory and her chain-of-command while so close to her retirement. I ended up helping her photo access problem on her computer, and then left.

The days and weeks that followed were difficult. My supervisor became distant and oddly demanding. Her behavior didn't make sense. Suddenly she seemed like a micro-manager and yet she avoided me.

The MSGT was having medical problems – needing ear surgery – so he was away from the Armory quite a bit. I kept track of his schedule as well as I could – and avoided being in his presence.

CHAPTER 6
Discredit the Employee

My elbow continued to be painful. I was placed on and off of modified duty. It was difficult to coordinate medical issues with my Supervisor as she remained detached and unapproachable.

Adding to the tension between us was my discovery that she had changed my timesheet, removing the overtime I had worked at her request.

At first I thought it had been an error at the Puzzle Palace, but after comparing notes with the financial clerk, it was clear that the overtime had not been turned on my time sheet.

My supervisor had not been aware that she was supposed to get permission to work me overtime. When she turned in my timesheet with overtime, it was kicked back. Instead of telling me about her mistake, she changed my timesheet.

When confronted with the fact, my Supervisor said that we would "work it out" – that she would give me extra time off to make it up. I told her that I didn't want "under the table" compensation, I wanted and needed the money that I had earned.

Coworkers noticed the change in our relationship. The D Company Readiness NCO came to me, openly upset about the rift in our friendship.

"You got to talk to her, she's your friend!" he counseled.

"I tried to talk to her," I replied. "She acts like she doesn't want to deal with me."

"But she's your friend...."

"I'm not so sure she wants to be my friend. She's between a rock and a hard place and doing the right thing, like she always talks about doing, is not easy for her right now. She's kind of in the hot-seat with human resources too."

He pressed me to tell him more, but I cut the conversation short.

"I can't do anything to make her be my friend or do right by me. Maybe the stress of the S-4 job is taking its toll on her, but it wasn't me who stopped trying to be friends. The ball is in her court."

Adding to the stress of her job, my Supervisor no longer asked me to help her type and pour over lists and do other tasks. She was on her own.

Another paycheck went by without the return of my overtime. I realized that my Supervisor was simply not going to own up to her mistake and do something to see that I was paid for working overtime.

Instead, on a Friday she called me into her office and presented me with paperwork, a negative performance appraisal, a document stating my work hours, and a statement ordering me to give her my Armory keys.

While I did have a performance plan, she had never gone over the plan with me as required. I suddenly realized that she thought having me sit in her office and list on her calendar tasks I had accomplished was a "performance plan."

The negative appraisal did not reference my actual performance plan – it was simply a negative review out of the blue. The document stating my work hours was based on my work hours from three years prior with an hour for lunch. When I had moved to my farm, it was too far to go home for lunch, so I switched to a half hour lunch which allowed me to go home earlier in the day.

I told her I was not signing the documents because they were inaccurate. She became upset and tried to force me to sign the documents and to give her my keys.

Her demand that I relinquish my Armory keys to her was in direct violation of what the Key Control Sergeant had told me when I signed for the keys.

"It is only for the weekend." She said. "I will return your keys to you on Monday, but you won't have the master key anymore."

"You aren't key control." I said. "I signed for those keys and I need them to get into the building and access offices and do my job."

"This is for your own protection." She insisted. "Give me the keys."

It occurred to me that stress may have pushed her over the edge – she was shorter than I was, but I had seen her knock out pushups with the best of the male soldiers – and she was trained in hand-to-hand combat. I was no match for her if she became physical.

I unclipped the keys that had been issued to me from my belt loop and one-by-one dropped them into her hand.

"This is wrong, you know." I said, fighting back tears. "This is in violation of your own military rules."

"I'm a civilian just like you." She replied.

That made no sense. The thirteen full-timers at the Armory prided themselves on being federally funded soldiers, holding coveted full-time positions, unlike the "Citizen Soldiers" who held civilian jobs in the communities and only became soldiers two days a month and two weeks a year for training.

After taking my keys she pointed to the documents and said, "Now sign these."

"No. Those documents are incorrect – and you still owe me my overtime pay. Is that why you doing this?" I asked.

Fear flickered in her eyes briefly. She clamped her lips shut and picked up the documents angrily.

"You'll get most of your keys back on Monday morning. Now go home. You're dismissed."

Over the weekend it occurred to me that perhaps the chain of command above my Supervisor felt that without a building access key, I wouldn't be able to work overtime. Although I had stayed late at my Supervisor's request, she was not willing to own up to the fact.

I did receive my keys back Monday morning. The master key had been replaced with individual keys to offices, mechanical room, and classrooms. I had an impressive bunch of keys to pack around and sort through when unlocking a door.

In time, I thought, my pay would be straightened out – and at least, I wasn't being flashed by the MSGT who had undergone ear surgery and was out on sick leave – or so I thought.

One morning the D Company Readiness NCO told me that there was a fluorescent light that burning out that he would show me later that morning.

I headed out of my office with my janitors cart and chuckled to myself. My overloaded key ring jingled even louder than the rattle of the cart.

"Donna." I heard a male voice call me.

Thinking that it was the D Company NCO, I left my cart and walked toward the sound of the voice coming from the entryway to the male bunkroom.

As I stepped into the entryway, the MSGT stepped out of the shadows, shorts down, masturbating.

I drew in my breath, backed up and when I turned to run lost my footing. It felt like my nightmares where I tried to run from some unknown danger.

The MSGT laughed as I managed to exit the entryway and run up the hallway – running into and almost knocking over the D Company Readiness NCO.

"Donna! What's wrong?!" He asked, alarmed.

I wanted to tell him what the MSGT had done to me, but he was already experiencing discrimination – and I believed his immediate reaction would be to confront the MSGT, possibly with a fist. He would run the risk of killing his career.

"I just…um…" I faltered, wishing I could blurt out everything about the ongoing sexual harassment by the MSGT, but I couldn't let him do something rash. "I…just…I…spider…" and then quickly changing the subject, "You told me that you wanted to show me a problem with a light?"

He gave me an odd look. I was usually the one called upon to remove mice, bugs, and once even a snake from the Armory.

"In here." He said as he pushed open the door and called out the words I always said before entering the men's restroom. "Hello, is anyone in here?"

There was no answer, so he led the way to a light that was dim and flickering just above a sink. "It's hard seeing to shave." He said.

" It could be a failing ballast, but I'll try changing the tube." I said. "Thank you for showing it to me. If replacing the tube doesn't help, I'll put in a work order."

As I spoke, the door leading from the male locker room into the restroom opened. The MSGT walked in with a towel over his shoulder.

I felt the color leave my face. "Thanks again for showing me the light – I'll take care if it right away."

Leaving the two soldiers in the restroom, I hurried to my Supervisor's office. She wasn't there. Even if she had been there, I doubted that she would want to hear what I had to tell her.

I found a sticky-note and a pen and jotted, "It happened again." She would know what I meant.

My left elbow had been experiencing increasingly severe tendon pain. I'd had the maximum allowed two cortisone injections and remained on modified duty, transferring much of the workload to my right arm.

My doctor said the best option was surgery and that it should be scheduled soon to avoid permanent damage. My Supervisor would simply have to quit avoiding me and do her part in arranging for me to take medical leave.

I found her in the Armory kitchen making hard boiled eggs. It looked as though she had been crying. When I told her about needing elbow surgery, she unexpectedly gave me a hug and said, "I'm glad we are talking again."

Startled, I replied, "You are my friend."

Surgery was scheduled for the following week, but the problem of my overtime remained unsolved. Human Resources had called me asking for details of my having worked overtime. After explaining, I was told that it would be taken care of, but several pay periods had passed without compensation for overtime.

Frustrated, I called the Department of Labor to ask what I should do. I had kept the chain-of-command rule, going to my Supervisor directly and repeatedly. I thought perhaps DOL would have a suggestion.

Instead of advising me, DOL jumped immediately into action. Heads apparently began to roll.

While I was buffing the drill floor, my Supervisor told me she needed me in her office. I left the buffer had followed her to her office.

"We are going to have a tele-conference with the Armory Commander and straighten this all out."

"Straighten what out?" I asked.

"You were not authorized to work overtime!" shouted the Commander's voice from the speaker phone.

"I was asked to work overtime..." I looked at my Supervisor, "By my..."

"No you weren't." the Commander cut me off. "You were not authorized and furthermore..."

My Supervisor was nervously fumbling with what looked like a Performance Appraisal sheet in her hand.

"No. Not again." I said. "Whenever you folks make mistakes or drop the ball, you try and save face by blaming and discrediting the employee. It's not going to happen today. I want union representation." I spoke calmly and stated my rights under the bargaining agreement..

The state maintenance workers union had recently been authorized and the contract ratified. I turned to leave.

"You don't have a union!" the Armory commander's voice was surprisingly loud for coming through the phone's speakers.

I quietly went back to the drill floor and continued buffing.

At the end of the day, my Supervisor handed me a formal letter ordering me to be present at a meeting on Thursday with my union representative present.

"Be at this meeting or you will face disciplinary measures."

Thursday after lunch, the union's chief steward for the area and the regional manager arrived at the Armory for the meeting. My supervisor seemed flustered and hurried us into place at the Commander's big conference table.

Several people from the Puzzle Palace were present – the head of Human Resources, my Human Resources person, and a lady I had never met. As it turned out, the lady was with the Department of Labor.

The Armory Commander, my Supervisor and a young Armory Private joined us around the table.

My Supervisor began by handing a Performance Appraisal to the folks from Human Resources.

"It looks here as though you have been failing..."

"Excuse me, but may I ask," broke in the Union Regional Manager, "...is there a record of counseling prior to issuing a negative Appraisal?"

My Human Resources person, knowing that he was right, quietly tucked the Appraisal under her notebook and said, "Ok, let's start fresh."

The meeting ended with me agreeing to call the Department of Labor and waive my right to receiving pay for working overtime – this was in exchange for the promise of being treated like the military folks I worked with. When they had days off – I would have a day off. When they had parties or events during work hours I could participate without taking leave.

"Wouldn't you like to be treated like everyone else and be a part of the team?" was the question posed by my Human Resources person that caused me to relent and agree to forget about the money owed me.

After the Human Resources and DOL folks left, the meeting continued.

I was told that when I returned from my medical leave, I would have a new supervisor – the male NCO from the PAC office. I was told that I would have to begin clocking in and out with a time clock and before it arrived I had to physically tell my Supervisor I was arriving or leaving work.

Because there was a good chance of my being on medical leave for over a month, I was told to turn my keys in to key control – which was standard procedure.

The time clock idea seemed a bit paranoid, but I liked the idea – it would keep my Supervisor honest.

I was glad for my elbow surgery on Monday – I was glad to get away from the Armory. I was getting a new supervisor, and perhaps the MSGT would be gone when I got back.

"Donna, wait a minute."

I turned to see the PAC Sergeant who was to be my new Supervisor.

" I hope all goes well with your surgery. I'm looking forward to working with you. Under my supervision, I believe you will be the best state employee."

CHAPTER 7
Medical Leave

My elbow surgery went well, but I was not allowed to return to work on modified duty – I had to wait until I was totally healed and ready for full duty.

During the time I was on medical leave, I had to fill out timesheets and use a certain amount of my own sick leave so the state would continue to pay their potion of my health insurance premiums.

When I stopped by the Armory every two weeks, it was clear that the MSGT was still working there.

As time came closer to return to work, I began having even more difficulty sleeping. Nightmares were frequent. I would wake up in the morning with my teeth clenched and my muscles tense.

When my doctor returned me to full use of my arm, he told me he was having me return to work in two weeks.

"I want you to start using your arm as you do things around your farm." He told me as he wrote the return to work order. "After you've been back to work for two weeks I'll see you one last time and then most likely cut you loose."

"What's wrong?" he asked as he handed me the order.

A wave of panic washed over me as he said the words "back to work."

"Doc, I'm afraid to go back. I have a weaker arm now, and I can't defend myself.

I had seen a news program about a sex offender who started out by just peeking into windows and ended up committing rape and murder. The MSGT's behavior had gone from flashing me to trapping me and forcing me to watch him masturbate. He was escalating. I feared what he would do next.

"Why are you afraid?" He asked, puzzled.

I took a deep breath and told him what the MSGT had been doing to me and that my Supervisor hadn't done anything to help me or make him stop and the MSGT was still at the Armory...and

"You need to go to the police."

"They'll fire me."

"They can't fire you for going to the police." He reassured. "You need protection. Go to the police."

It took me almost the entire two weeks to gather the courage to go to the police. Sometimes I would wonder

62

if maybe I was just being paranoid, maybe being flashed wasn't as bad as I thought it was. But in the long run, I knew my doctor was right – I had to seek police protection.

After stacking firewood one day I made a list of dates and times that I had marked on my calendar and headed for the Air Base. The Air Force Security Forces provided police protection for the National Guard Armory, a "tenant" on base.

PART III
Retaliation

*

CHAPTER 8
Seeking Police Protection

The desk sergeant's eyes widened slightly as he repeated what I had just told him, "You need to report sexual harassment in the National Guard Armory?"

Panic welled up inside me. I could still walk out of the cop shop and take my chances.

"Maybe I better think about this." I said, glancing at the door. "They'll fire me if I..."

"Ma'am, it's okay. Let me call someone who can help you decide."

On cue, a uniformed Security Police sergeant appeared and said, "Ma'am, would you like to come with us and tell us what's going on?" He smiled and pointed to a room down the hallway where a female wearing plain clothes stood by a door.

I felt fear wash over me. I wanted to run. How could I tattle on the National Guard? They got upset if I broke my chain-of-command. They would be furious! But how could I go back into that disgusting and dangerous situation? I had to report the crimes against me – for my safety.

"Yes." I said and walked into the room. "I'll file a report."

Still fearful, I didn't give the perpetrator's name as I told what he had been doing to me.

One of the investigators said, "We may know who you are talking about. We confiscated a soldier's work computer because he was storing pornography on it...."

"Oh, no!" I broke in emphatically. "That's not the man who is flashing me – that's my new supervisor – the Air Force took away his computer for a month because of pornography. It was joked about in Monday morning meetings."

The investigators exchanged a look. The female investigator said softly, "We want to help you, but we can't unless you tell us who is harassing you."

I knew she was right.

"Okay. I'll tell you everything – names and all."

It took several hours to describe what the Master Sergeant had done to me. After telling the investigators everything I could remember verbally, I had to fill out a handwritten complaint form. When I finished my hand hurt from gripping the pen tightly as I wrote. I felt emotionally drained.

"Ma'am, do you know if the soldiers at the National Guard Armory are active duty?

I thought for a minute and answered, "They call themselves 'full timers' and a portion of federal funds pays them, but they are under a State UCMJ code."

In my searching to find my own employment information, I had discovered that the National Guard had their own Uniform Code of Military Justice which mirrored the Federal UCMJ. They were governed by the same rules of conduct, but under State authority.

"Thank you, ma'am, we will look into it. Now, here is information for you." He said as he handed me a Victim's Rights brochure. "There are phone numbers you can call for support. It is your right as the victim to remain informed during the investigation and know exactly what happens to the perpetrator. Do you understand?"

I nodded and took the pamphlets he was handing me.

"The first thing we will do is inform the Armory Commander about the actions of the MSGT under his command."

My face must have reflected the sudden fear I felt. He continued, "Don't worry we are here to protect you. Here is my card. If you have any questions or more information don't hesitate to call me."

I walked out of the cop shop feeling relieved that I was not alone any longer, but with a knot in my stomach – by seeking police protection, I had gone past my Supervisor and my chain of command.

CHAPTER – 9
Return to the Armory

After a weekend of worry, I returned to work on Monday, a few days after having gone to the Air Force Police. I walked into my office and stopped in my tracks at the open door.

I expected a mess after three months of people using the supplies and equipment, but my chemical locker had been removed and the contents of the locker sat on the floor. The posters and information that had been on and in the chemical locker lay in a pile on my desk.

The shelves of supplies had obviously been rummaged through – used but reusable buffer pads were gone. I had saved hundreds of dollars by rinsing and reusing floor buffer pads.

Startled I noticed that the handle on my office door had been replaced with a round doorknob – with no lock. How would I secure the chemicals and equipment I was signed for?

I walked to my desk and sat down. The lock on my desk was broken and drawers had been rifled through. The Building Information ring binder I had been keeping since day-one was gone. I had been compiling the information book to make it easy for whoever may take my place when I moved up within State Civil Service. All my records, recycling information, contact numbers and personal information on classes and training was missing.

Uneasily, I thumbed through the stack of posters and information sheets that had been on my chemical locker. The photograph of the man with an American flag across his back was not in the jumbled pile of papers.

Feeling violated and angry I began setting my office back in order, making mental notes for what I would say at the Monday Morning Meeting.

My new Supervisor poked his head in my office door, "Welcome back, Donna. Right after the Monday meeting we'll sit down and go over your Performance Plan together. I've taken State Supervisor training, and as you know, that's the way to start off on the right foot." He smiled.

"Ok, that will be great." I replied. He had said that he wanted to be a good supervisor and help me be the best ever employee. I hurried to clean the Armory restrooms before the meeting started.

As I walked to the Monday Morning Meeting, my Supervisor stopped me in the rotunda and said, "We have to change our Performance Plan meeting to One O'clock this afternoon. The Commander wants to meet with us."

A feeling of uncertainty stabbed through my stomach. "Usually Performance Plan meetings are between Supervisor and Employee." I said.

"I know." He replied. "But the new Commander wants to be there for the meeting."

"New Commander?" I asked, my anxiety rising. "What happened to...."

"He's not here any longer." He cut my question short. "Just be at the Commander's office by One O'clock."

The Monday Morning Meeting was emceed by the new Commander who seemed somewhat ill at ease while speaking in front of people. He kept clearing his throat and searching for words.

When it was my turn to speak at the end of the meeting, I asked, "Has anyone seen my big ring binder titled 'Building Information?' It was in my desk before I went on leave."

"What does it look like?" The Recruiter asked, looking up from his notepad. I described the ring binder in detail. Several people hurriedly scribbled notes, obviously taking my dilemma seriously.

The Recruiter stopped writing and looked up suddenly. Addressing the PFC who had been helping my old Supervisor, he asked, "Have you seen her book? You've been handing the recycling program while Donna was out on leave."

The PFC shrugged his shoulders and shook his head, his cheeks turning bright red.

Skipping lunch, I continued cleaning the Armory. It was apparent that nobody had attempted to clean during my absence. I hated seeing the building in such a state of disarray and filth.

When it was time for the Performance Plan meeting, I took a quick drink of water to quiet my growling stomach, grabbed a notebook and went to the Commander's office.

The new Commander was sitting down behind his desk. My Supervisor, standing beside a chair motioned me to take a seat. His face looked a little flushed but in a most cordial tone of voice he sat down and began the meeting.

"Ok, here is your current Performance Plan." He said handing me and the Commander each a copy. "We will go over every detail and we will all sign the Plan."

My Performance Plan was for the most part unchanged, for daily, weekly and monthly duties, but when we reached the portion describing my Recycling Program, I said, "Just a minute – most of the program is missing."

The Commander cleared his throat and said, "No this is how it will be from now on."

"But all the records and turning in the materials to the proper places – and inspections...."

"The PFC will be taking care of that." The Commander broke in impatiently. "You will pick up the trash."

"But I..."

My Supervisor cut me off, "Let's move on. We are almost done."

The very last paragraph of the Performance Plan had a new statement added. My supervisor read, "*Any and all issues or grievances will go through myself or the Commander prior to leaving this facility.*"

"What do you mean?" I asked.

My Supervisor answered, "You will bring all matters to us first. You will not contact any Air Force entity directly, especially the Security Police."

"You're telling me that I'm not to, like, call an ambulance if somebody gets hurt? So if you fall out," I looked at the Commander, "You want me to run and get my Supervisor instead of dialing 911?"

"That's right." He replied curtly.

"You had better check with Human Resources about that – it is not an appropriate mandate to include in my Performance Plan"

I had a strong feeling being banned from interaction with the Air Force was in direct response to his having been informed by the Security Police about the MSGT's bad behavior.

After the meeting was over the two men took me on a tour of the Armory. We walked through the hallways, and rooms while they pointed out cobwebs, dirt and disarray.

The Commander told me that the building was not acceptable and in a condescending tone of voice told me how to do my job – the job that I had been doing well for many years.

Fighting back tears, tried changing the focus by asking if I should go to key control and get my keys back.

"No." the Commander replied almost sarcastically. "You won't get any keys back. If you need a door unlocked, find a key holder to open it for you. And you are not to go into the S-2 office at all."

My Supervisor's eyes darted to the Commander's face briefly. The Commander ignored him. S-2 was where the MSGT's desk was.

"Um, the keys - that's going to be difficult." I said, thinking about the toilet paper and paper towel dispensers. I was the only one who had those keys.

The Commander's face twisted into a sneer "Well that's your problem." He replied, his voice getting louder. "Also, you will adhere to your schedule as stated in your Performance Plan. You will not participate in Armory events."

"But my Human Resources person said specifically at the meeting before my surgery that I was supposed to be treated just like you military folks in exchange for my waiving the pay due me."

"Well I wasn't at that meeting and this is my Armory now." The Commander shouted at me.

Tears filled my eyes and spilled down my cheeks.

My supervisor said sternly, "Donna, you are just going to have to get thicker skin."

I turned and ran down the hall toward my office fighting back sobs.

Over the following week, I felt singled out. Coworkers who before had chatted easily with me as I made my rounds picking up trash and recyclable items from their offices quietly avoided looking at me.

Only the D Company Readiness NCO remained on friendly terms. He told me that the Armory personnel had been given orders not to talk to me.

"Why?" I asked him.

Frowning, he replied, "I don't know."

I tried to avoid asking anyone to unlock a door for me, instead I waited until a room was in use, and then quickly vacuumed or picked up trash. I placed toilet paper and paper towels on top of the locked dispensers. When I did have to ask someone to unlock a door, it was an obvious irritation.

My Supervisor was difficult to read. Sometimes he was cheerful and almost friendly – other times he was as cold and silent as my coworkers.

When my Supervisor was in a cheerful mode, I asked if I could have my recycling program duties back once I had returned the Armory to good condition.

"I think that will be all right" he told me. "Come and ask me again in a couple more weeks."

The glimmer of hope encouraged me.

"Oh, and I need you to sign something." He handed me the last page of my Performance Plan. The paragraph forbidding me to contact the Air Force had been lined out. "Human Resources said you were right about this." Initial right by the paragraph I struck out. I'll give you a copy."

Two weeks later I had the Armory back to its spit and polished shiny floors, gleaming fixtures – I felt proud once again of the building. I approached my Supervisor and asked if I could have my recycling job duties back.

"I'll ask the Commander." He replied.

"You are my Supervisor, it's your call to make." I continued. "I plan on going back to college to pursue Environmental Science training, and the State will reimburse part of my tuition fee if I have environmental job duties. It also helps my elbows to have recordkeeping type tasks to do."

"Your elbows, plural?" he quizzed.

"Yes." I confessed. "The hallways and drill floor were in very bad shape, and the humidity has been high making the dust mop stick to the floor surface. It is difficult to push the mop when it sticks and rolls up. I've strained my right elbow."

A glimmer of delight briefly passed across his face before he spoke. "We may need a statement from you saying that you can't do your job...."

I cut him off, "That is not what I said. My right elbow hurts from pushing too hard on the mop and babying the arm that had surgery. I go back to the doctor in a few days for my final post op appointment."

I glanced around me. "Look at the Armory – it's back up to standard. My recycle duties...."

"I'll ask the Commander." He broke in, "But don't get your hopes up. But about keys, we're giving you office keys and paper dispenser keys. It's too hard for people to have to cater to you when you need doors unlocked."

He may as well have slapped my face – them cater to me? It was never my idea to have to ask people to unlock doors. Obviously my coworkers had complained.

76

A month after my return to the Armory, the PFC who had been doing my recycling duties said something in a Monday morning meeting that caught my attention. He quoted something I had written and placed in my Building Information ring binder. The only way he could have known to say what he did was if he had seen my missing binder.

I went to the acting S-4 Sergeant and told him I suspected his PFC knew where my Building Information binder was.

"Did you look in his desk?" the Sergeant asked.

"Of course not!" I replied. "I'll dust shelves and personal areas when asked, but I don't touch people's desks."

"Well I will." He replied, and began pulling open drawers.

A jar of peanut butter, crumpled potato chip bags, the last of a loaf of bread – and there underneath the mess was my missing binder.

"He lied to my face!" I said as I clutched the ring binder to my chest. "I asked him if he had seen it in doing my recycling program and he said he hadn't."

Later that afternoon I confronted the PFC, "We found my missing ring binder in your desk – why did you lie?"

Looking as though he were ready to throw up, the PFC looked at the floor and said, "It was given to me. I was supposed to use it."

"By who?" I demanded

"Uh, I'll get in trouble if I say." He replied.

77

"Well I'll go to the Commander and tell him you stole my binder if you don't say." I said angrily.

"He knows."

"What? How...you mean...." I frowned.

"Ya," he nodded. "He gave your book to me."

Suddenly the pieces fell together. The Commander and my Supervisor had removed the chemical locker, pilfered through my office and my desk, stole the binder that obviously was important to me doing my job.

Their answer to my having been locked in my office was not to remove the MSGT, their friend, but to remove the lock from my office door.

"Hello, this is Donna." I recognized the caller ID as the Air Force Investigator handling my complaint of sexual harassment. True to their word, the Air Force Police kept me informed on the status of their investigation.

I had been informed when the MSGT was brought in for questioning, and at first had lied and denied everything. When a physical examination proved that he did indeed have the birthmark on his private parts that I had described, he confessed.

Cell phone pressed to my ear, I was eager for updated information.

"Ma'am, I'm afraid I have bad news for you." Said the Investigator. "The Air Force doesn't have jurisdiction in this case."

My heart sank as he described the difference between UCMJ Title 10 and Title 32 and then concluded, "Only the State Adjutant General can investigate and prosecute crimes that occur inside a National Guard Armory."

"If the crime had occurred on the lawn outside the Armory, the Air Force would have jurisdiction, but all we could do was ban the perpetrator from entering the Air Base. We took that action to protect you, and we have passed the case along to the National Guard – the unit's Battalion (BN) Commander."

My dismay melted. The BN Commander was the Colonel who had moved the micro-managing Armory Commander to an out-of-the-way office. The BN Commander was hated and feared by my coworkers for being exacting and demanding – but I respected the man. He was no-nonsense and hard charging. I hung up the phone feeling confident that the BN Commander would again do right by me.

"Donna." I jumped and spun around. "You sure are touchy." said my Supervisor, looking at me with open disapproval. "You need to change the burned out light tubes in the male locker room. It's so dark in there we can barely see."

"Okay, I'll get right on it." I answered, trying not to let my hurt feelings show. I wanted people to like me and to recognize the quality of my work.

With my aluminum step ladder under one arm and a box of light tubes in my hand, went to the locker room.

"Is anyone in there?" I yelled into the open door.

No one answered so I walked in and set the ladder and lights down. Then I taped a well-used sign on the door that read, "WORKING INSIDE - DO NOT ENTER."

Whenever I worked in the male restroom, locker room or bunk room I posted the warning.

The dimly lit room was eerie. It looked as though half of the lights indeed were burned out. Apparently while I was on medical leave, nobody had attempted any minor maintenance.

"I'll soon fix that." I thought to myself as I began the tedious process of dragging the ladder to burned out lights, opening fixtures, extracting sometimes corroded burned out tubes and replacing them with fresh ones.

To avoid extra trips up and down the ladder, I pushed the box of new lights up on top of a row of lockers. After removing a burned out tube, I set it on top of the lockers and my jaw dropped. I pulled my hand back so quickly I almost fell off the ladder.

I had placed my hand on a pile of very graphic hard core pornographic magazines, knocking them to the floor.

"Oh gross!" I exclaimed shaking my hand as though to remove the filth.

I couldn't leave the magazines all over the floor, so I climbed down the ladder and scooped them back into a pile, shocked at the images of women being portrayed as sexual playthings. After shoving them back on top of the locker, I headed toward my Supervisor's office.

When I reported what had happened, my Supervisor laughed and said, "I know what you are talking about – I'll take care of it."

That was the first time I had ever seen pornography in the Armory – but it wasn't the last.

I began finding pornographic magazines in offices, in the male bunkroom, on the floor of stalls in the male restroom and even on my own janitor's cart. Remembering my former Supervisor's mandate that I have "proof," of what the MSGT was doing to me. I began photographing the offensive materials for "proof."

CHAPTER 10
Adverse Actions

I was beginning to hate the job I had once loved.

The Armory Commander either ignored me as though I didn't exist, or he spoke harshly seeming to enjoy watching tears fill my eyes.

My Supervisor usually was stern with me, but on occasion displayed cheerfulness. I learned to dread his good moods as they preceded negative actions toward me.

I learned to be quiet about my likes and dislikes. Tasks I enjoyed doing were taken away and unsavory tasks were added to my workload. Along with my recycling duties I had enjoyed planting and maintaining the Armory flowerbeds. Quietly I watched as the Commander ordered soldiers to tear out the flowerbeds and turn them into lawn.

I felt watched. One afternoon while cleaning baseboards in a hallway, out of the corner of my eye I saw a face staring at me from behind the doorway window. When I turned to look, the face disappeared. Frequently I would catch a fleeting glimpse of a person watching me.

The increased workplace stress prompted me to quietly apply for other state jobs. I was vested for retirement with the State and didn't want to lose the time I had invested.

I interviewed for a job at a Veterans Cemetery and was sorely disappointed to come in second for the position. Digging graves sounded far more desirable that the workplace I was experiencing.

Working under physical and emotional tension had negative effects on my body. Like a scared rabbit, my muscles were always tight, ready to run. Fatigue, fear and physical effort were taking their toll.

My right thumb throbbed from gripping the floor buffer and vacuum cleaner. I was having trouble operating the floor machines and holding a pen and writing was also painful.

One day my Disability Attorney called to tell me the status on my left elbow surgery compensation. He advised me to report my hurting thumb to my Supervisor without delay.

I also shared with him what was happening to me in my workplace. I told him briefly about the sexual harassment by the MSGT, and what I was experiencing after having gone to the police.

"You are describing a hostile work environment." He said without hesitation. "You need to find a Human Rights A ttorney to help you."

Once again I turned to the Union for assistance and was referred to a law firm in a nearby city. After a brief telephone interview, I was invited to come in and fill out paperwork – they would take my case.

Immediately I felt safer. I began communicating on a regular basis with an attorney who assured me that what was happening to me was neither legal nor my fault. I was no longer alone.

I reported my thumb to my Supervisor as required by State employment rules, and was sent to a work-comp doctor who prescribed a thumb brace. The brace helped a little, but in turn put more pressure on my right elbow.

When I reported my declining elbow to my Supervisor he seemed happy to fill out a work injury form and set up a doctor's appointment for me.

"I may want you to write out all the things that you can't do anymore." My Supervisor said, in a cooperative tone that raised a red flag in my mind.

"I can do my job." I replied hurriedly. "I just find different ways to accomplish tasks and I get my job done."

"We'll see about that." He replied looking pleased with himself.

Two days later my Supervisor handed me a formal letter mandating that I appear at a meeting at 11 o clock Friday morning. "Oh, and Donna, he said smiling "You will want to have your Union Representative with you at the meeting."

My Union Representative and I were seated at the Commanders big conference table. My Supervisor and a female soldier who I had never met sat across from us.

My Supervisor handed us each a copy of a document and said, "Okay are you ready? I will read this out loud:

1. This is notice that I propose to suspend you from your position without pay for thirty (30) work days.

2. The reason for the proposed suspension is because of conduct by yourself that is unbecoming a state employee due to immoral, indecent and disgraceful conduct. Conduct unbecoming a state employee came to my attention when presented with an investigation from the Air Force Office of Special Investigation (AFOSI). The conduct is detailed below."

My Supervisor read subparagraphs a and b, in which he had mixed bits and pieces of my police report all jumbled together – making it sound as though all the flashing and masturbating assaults by the MSGT had happened in the course of one day rather than over an entire year.

"You got that all wrong...." I started to say, but my Supervisor cut me off.

"Let me finish reading this and then you can have your turn."

3. The proposed adverse action is appropriate. The rationale behind the proposed suspension is simple: the conduct annotated above shows behavior that will not be tolerated. The Army National Guard is an organization that is founded on discipline and order. Your actions involving the MSGT are irreprehensible. Due to the severity of this incident a suspension is warranted.

4. You have a right to review all evidence and material relied on for this adverse action. All evidence and material used as a basis for the suspension is attached.

5. You have the right to reply to this adverse action. This reply gives you the opportunity to discuss the action with an official who is knowledgeable about the incident and has the authority to decide if the action should be sustained.

6. You have the right to an excused absence to prepare your reply. Contact myself to coordinate the appropriate absence. Four to eight hours is normally sufficient to prepare a reply.

7. The Armory Commander will issue an original decision at the earliest practical date after receipt of replies or after the reply period has ended. Be advised if the proposed action is upheld by the deciding official it will be affected on the date established in the original decision."

Attached to the proposed adverse action was a copy of my handwritten police report.

"First of all," I said, trying hard to control my breathing, "You got the facts wrong! Nobody ever asked ME what the MSGT has done to me, And...."

My supervisor interrupted, "This proposed suspension is based solely on your own police report...

"Well you got the facts wrong!" I said. "A sixth – grader could compare what I wrote and what you wrote and see that the two accounts are totally different."

My Union Representative broke in asking, "Are you familiar with the Whistleblower Act?"

"Um, no." answered my supervisor, blinking innocently.

"For the record," I spoke again. "I am going to tell all three of you exactly what the MSGT did to me...."

After I finished describing the sexual harassment in detail, my Supervisor said, "I'm really sorry that happened to you – nobody should have to go through all that."

He paused and continued, "But, I am going to have to recommend the suspension anyway. It's almost noon - you can have the rest of the day off to prepare your response."

At home, with no appetite for lunch, I called my attorney.

"What?" he exclaimed. "That's hard to believe! You need to follow through with your response. Ask your Union Representative for help with filing a grievance and we will see if they actually go through with the proposed action."

I was working on my response to the proposed adverse action when the phone rang.

"Hello, I need someone to mow my lawn right away!" said the female voice when I answered the phone.

"My husband is deployed, I live on base, I'm pregnant and my grass is too long – I'm going to get written up."

The Air Force base did indeed have grass inspectors who went out with rulers - if grass measured over 4 inches high, occupants of quarters were written up. Families had been kicked out of government quarters for long grass.

"Ma'am, I'm in the middle of an important project right now, but I can come out tomorrow morning...."

"No, I'm not... uh, I can't be here tomorrow, and I have a corner yard, and the grass inspectors will write me up." The lady begged. "Please can you come out and mow for me right now. I'm desperate!"

I looked at the clock. It was mid afternoon. I would have to hurry.

"Ok, I have to hook my truck up to my mower trailer and get fuel – it'll take me about an hour to get there, but I'll help you out." I said as I walked to the kitchen to fill my water jug. "Give me your address."

The last thing I felt like doing was mow a lawn, but how could I turn her down.

I was halfway to the Air Base when I realized that I had left my thumb brace on the kitchen counter. If I went back to get the brace, I would run out of daylight. Oh well, mowing and weed-eating didn't stress my thumb like buffing floors.

The lady's yard was indeed a challenge. The grass was long and wet. The gate leading into the tiny back yard was too narrow for my ride on mower to fit through, so I had to use my temperamental old push mower.

When I finally finished, I looked around at the neatly mowed yard and thought, "I really should be taking before and after photos of yards for advertising."

After loading my equipment, I didn't have to knock on the door – the lady stepped out of her house and handed me thirty dollars in cash.

Normally I would have charged more, for the extra work of push mowing the back yard and making many more passes with the big mower to mulch up the clumps of cut grass, but I smiled, thanked the lady and handed her a business card.

I spent the weekend preparing my reply to my Supervisor's letter. I felt confident that hearing what had happened to me at the hands of the MSGT, the proposed adverse action would be dropped. I was so wrong!

I was accused of having participated in the sexual harassment. Despite my efforts, I was suspended thirty days without pay, as my supervisor said, "based solely on my police report."

My attorney told me it was time to take action – we filed a complaint of sexual harassment with the Equal Employment Opportunity Commission. The wheels of justice slowly began turning.

My right elbow had become extremely painful. Surgery was recommended. I was assigned a State caseworker who made all appointments for me and went with me to every post-op doctor's appointment. My Disability Attorney told me caseworkers testify against employees at the final hearing and cautioned me to be careful.

The four-month recovery period at home was a dark time. I struggled to make ends meet on Workman's Compensation pay. I couldn't trust my caseworker, my Supervisor didn't hide his contempt for me when I turned in my timesheets and then my Disability Attorney telephoned me in anger.

"The Central Accident Reporting Office sent me a videotape of you mowing a lawn!" he shouted. "Someone is alleging that you are faking your elbow injuries! Do you know anything about this?!"

A weak, "No." was all I could manage to say. Then everything crashed in on me. I began sobbing.

I heard him clear his voice over the phone. "I didn't mean to upset you." He apologized, "It's just that, you were videotaped mowing a lawn – when were you mowing a lawn?"

I struggled to control the tears I had held back for so long. "I haven't mowed lawns since…" I struggled to remember. "…since they suspended me for going to the police."

"I mowed some lawns so I could pay my bills." Fear washed over me as I tried to think of where someone could possibly have secretly videotaped me.

"Look, I really am sorry." He apologized again. "I will get back to you."

After splashing my face with cold water I felt more composed. I called my Human Rights Attorney with the news of the secret videotape.

Realizing that I was being stalked, I began watching my surroundings carefully. I checked the back

91

seat of my car before getting in, I kept my farm dog near me while doing chores and at night I slept with a hammer under my pillow.

The day before I returned to work, I received a letter from the National Guard in the mail informing me that my work hours were being cut in half.

"What else can they possibly do to me?" I wondered.

CHAPTER 11
Grievances

The State Employee's Union with a newly ratified contract was eager to begin flexing its muscles. As a bargaining unit member, I had been encouraged to file a grievance regarding my job duties.

With the help of the area manager, I filled out a grievance form and presented it to my Supervisor, completing Step One.

Not surprisingly my Supervisor denied the request to return my environmental duties to me, sending the grievance to Step Two – the Armory Commander. The Commander's denial pushed the grievance to Step Three – the BN Commander.

Meeting with the BN Commander was encouraging. He listened to me carefully and seemed genuinely concerned about my needs.

I wondered about the investigation of the MSGT's sexual misconduct, but felt certain that I would be interviewed when the time was right. For the moment, the focus was on getting my environmental job duties back.

I was disappointed that the BN Commander did not return my job duties to me, but he praised me for my desire to continue my education and better myself.

The grievance was sent next to Human Resources person and finally to the Adjutant General.

The failure to successfully grieve my environmental job duties made me work even harder when I filed my second and even more important grievance – being suspended without pay.

This time my chain-of-command was changed, bypassing the BN Commander and instead going directly to Human Resources then to the Director over Human Resources before reaching the Adjutant General.

I was incredulous that nobody from the National Guard was able to understand that my Supervisor's proposal for my suspension was based on his gross misinterpretation of what I stated in my police report. My corrections of the information were ignored – everyone seemed determined to suspend me.

After the Adjutant General himself stated that I should suffer suspension in punishment for what they kept calling "my" actions, I had the option of seeking a hearing before an impartial judge.

But the State Commission on Human Rights had received my case information and after reviewing the details had granted me the right to a trial. My Attorney said that since we were planning on going to trial, we had to drop the grievance regarding my suspension without pay.

The third and final Union grievance I filed was regarding Doctor's Orders.

Prior to my second elbow surgery, my supervisor suddenly focused his attention on in my medical appointments and doctor's orders. He had difficulty understanding that each time I saw the doctor and was given instructions, the new doctor's order superseded the old order.

"Donna," My supervisor stopped me before the Monday Morning Meeting, "I want you to write out your doctor's orders in your own words and state that you concur with the doctor."

A red flag went up in my mind. "I'll need that in writing."

Without a word he turned and walked back into his office. After the meeting he handed me the mandate that I attach my interpretation of doctor's orders and the statement that I concur with the doctor. It read:

"Headquarters and Headquarters Company
To Donna J. Lindahl

Any time your bring me a note from a Medical doctor stating you are prohibited/limited from doing a task listed in your Performance Plan and Expectations, I need you to provide me with a letter either concurring or non-concurring with the doctor's notice."

"Okay. I'll get right on it." I said taking the memo from him.

I went to my office and wrote my rendition of what the doctor told me I could and couldn't do. At the bottom I wrote, "I will comply with my doctor's orders."

The next morning I arrived at work, sat at my desk. I was putting my purse in the bottom drawer when my Supervisor stormed into my office clearly angry.

"This is not what I asked you to do – are you so stupid that you can't obey a simple order..." he ranted, his mild speech impediment causing spit to sputter out of his mouth.

Terrified, I drew back in my chair as he shook a paper in my face.

"I told you to say that you 'concur' with your doctor!" he yelled. "You disobeyed my direct order!"

"I wrote that I will 'comply' with my doctor's orders..."

"That's not what I told you to do..." he continued yelling.

My fear gave way to hysteria. Despite myself I began laughing at my Supervisor.

My sudden detachment made him stop talking and look at me as though I were crazy.

"Your face is so red! You should see your face..." I babbled, laughing uncontrollably.

His rage diffused by my laughter, my Supervisor spun around on his heel and stormed out of my office, leaving me trembling uncontrollably.

The next day as I was dusting the drill floor my supervisor approached me to try again. "Donna I am not putting you in harm's way by asking you write that you concur or non-concur with your doctor."

"I'm sorry but I don't have medical training." I interrupted, "I am not qualified to concur with a doctor, but I have already said that I will comply with my doctor…"

"NO, that's not what I told you to do!" he shouted at me. "Your blatant disobedience is unacceptable!"

His rage and insistence that I use the word 'concur' frightened me. He had some agenda – some reason for wanting me to concur with a doctor and it was not for my benefit.

While he yelled, I fumbled for my cell phone and dialed my Union Representative.

"I can hear him," said my Representative. "Put him on the phone and I'll talk to him. And listen, for now, go ahead and write the word concur – we will grieve it."

I handed the phone to my Supervisor and after a while, he calmed down and handed the phone back to me.

"Your own Union Representative says you are supposed to write the word concur." He said looking pleased with himself.

"Yes." I replied. "I will write the word 'concur' and I will file a grievance."

Not surprisingly, my Supervisor denied my grievance at his Step One level. When I was called in to the Commander's office to receive his Step Two response I was glad my Union Representative was with me.

The Commander sat us down across his conference table. Shoving a thick black ring binder in front of me he said, "I'm giving this to the CARO (Central Accident Reporting Office) folks. Open it up. This is my response to your grievance."

The Response was a compilation of documents and notes (my Supervisor required every communication with him to be in writing), time sheets, doctor's orders, the photos of me posing on top of the bales of hay – all carefully organized with notes alleging that I was insubordinate and faking injuries to defraud the government.

As my Union Representative and I listened to the Commander, it was obvious that he had spent a great deal of time on and was very proud of his concerted effort to discredit and destroy me.

It was clear that the documents in the Commander's Response had been taken out of context and misinterpreted. I expected a negative response, but I hadn't expected him to compile a book.

The book, intended to damage me, surprisingly turned out to be helpful. I learned identity of the person who had secretly videotaped me mowing a lawn. Under Tab II Page 3 was a shocking memorandum:

MEMORANDUM FOR RECORD
SUBJECT: Fraudulent Worker's Compensation Claim Investigation

1. On 14 May 2004, between approximately 1800 and 1900 hours, I video taped MS. Donna J. Lindahl performing lawn maintenance duties at the residence of (name and address withheld).

2. In my personal investigation, I witnessed MS. Lindahl performing multiple lawn duties that, as her Supervisor at the Army National Guard Armory, know to be in direct violation of several doctor work orders. These duties include, but are not limited to, working without a prescribed arm brace, lifting in excess of 20 pounds, and using both arms in a repetitive motion while weed eating. She also used every bit of each arm and thumb to pull start a push mower, taking eight extremely hard pulls before the mower started. In addition, she has a pull start weed eater that took approximately five or six pulls before it started the first time and approximately 4 pulls the second time.

3. This statement is true. I have made this statement freely without hope of benefit or reward, without threat of punishment, and without coercion, unlawful influence, or unlawful inducement.

4. If you have questions concerning the above information, please contact me at (number withheld) or by email (email address withheld.)

Signed (name withheld)
Senior Personnel Supervisor

I was shocked. My Supervisor was the one who had secretly videotaped me. I didn't recognize the name or address where the video had been recorded, so I drove to the site.

As I approached the yard it all came back to me clearly – it was the pregnant lady's yard – the lady who begged me to come out immediately – just a few hours after I had received notice of my proposed suspension. My Supervisor had given me the afternoon off to work on my response – and so he could set me up to be secretly videotaped.

While I had forgotten my thumb brace, I had no restrictions for my right elbow. My Supervisor stalked and videotaped me a few days too early – I had not seen a doctor yet for my elbow. I was on full duty at work, and my while my elbow hurt when pushing the stubborn dust mop over the sticky floors, the totally different motions of mowing and weed eating did not cause elbow or thumb pain.

As usual, the grievance was denied all the way through the first three steps. My Union Representative accompanied me to the National Guard Puzzle Palace (State Headquarters) for a Step 4 hearing in front of a committee.

A retired Colonel in charge of Human Resources read the grievance aloud and after reviewing documents suggested, "Why don't you write that you will 'comply' with your doctor's orders."

Stunned, I said, "My supervisor yelled at me for saying I will 'comply' with my doctor."

The Colonel's face flushed briefly as he realized he had misunderstood the problem and had suggested in front of witness that I do what I had wanted to do all along.

I won the grievance!

In the grievance I suggested sending my Supervisor to anger management training. Being yelled at by him frightened and upset me.

A few days after winning the grievance, a Soldier who worked in my Supervisor's office took me aside, handed me a slip of paper with a phone number written on it and said, "Call me at home tonight. You need to know something."

Curious, I called the number after supper.

"Hi, this is Donna," I said when I heard the soldier answer his phone. "You have something to tell me?"

"Look, I just try to do my job and stay out of things at the Armory," he said, obviously nervous "But sometimes…well I'm a reserve police officer, and I know – I have to warn you."

"Warn me?" I asked.

"Yes ma'am. The Commander gave your Supervisor a piece of paper – some grievance you wrote – your Supervisor got really mad and…" he paused, taking a deep breath, "after he read it he said 'anger management! I'll show her anger management when I kill the fucking bitch!'"

Stunned I drew in my breath.

"I'm sorry, Ma'am I said it like he did. It just isn't right and, well, being a police officer, I knew I had to warn you." He finished.

"Thank you." I said weakly. "I appreciate it · I know it's dangerous for your career to warn me like this · I won't let them know. Thanks."

I hung up the phone. How far would my Supervisor's vengeance take him? I was in danger. The fear was real.

PART IV
Litigation

*

CHAPTER 12
Discovery

With a sigh of relief I pulled into a parking place and shut off the ignition. We had entered the "discovery" phase of gathering facts and I had to be at my Attorney's office in the heart of downtown for my deposition. I hate driving in the City. Tall buildings are majestic, but fast traffic, unexpected one-way streets and juggling a map while trying to read street signs stresses me – I prefer quiet country roads.

I was nervous about my deposition. I remember events in pictures and scenes – recalling names and dates is difficult. Depositions are like mini trials. The person being deposed is sworn to tell the truth, then both attorneys ask questions. Every word is carefully recorded by a court reporter.

My Attorney had petitioned for and received my entire personnel file from the State. He wanted me to review the file prior to my deposition. I hoped reading through the documents would refresh my memory and put me at ease.

"Here's a glass of water and a notepad," said my Attorney's Legal Assistant with a smile. "Read quickly, just skimming mostly, but pay attention to the pages we have marked with tabs – jot down anything that comes to mind about those entries."

I opened the cover of the four inch thick binder and began reading. Most of the documents I had seen before, but when I came to the first entry marked with a tab, my heart started beating faster. It was a section of email notes sent back and forth between my Supervisor and my Human Resources Person.

The first email was written by my Supervisor checking the validity of my last-minute announcement that I had to be at State Headquarters for a grievance meeting within a matter of hours.

My Human Resources Person wrote back to him saying that I did have a meeting and that she regretted having told me about it – the Union had not received the meeting information and if I had not attended the meeting, I would have automatically lost the grievance.

My Supervisor replied jokingly stating that she obviously was not too old to learn something. Then he wrote, "Enjoy your day with Ms Lindahl...I know I will enjoy my day without her."

Tears welled up in my eyes.

The next series of emails between my Supervisor and Human Resources Person was regarding my request to participate in the State's program sending its employees to help the people in Louisiana recover from Hurricane Katrina.

My Supervisor wrote that I had told him I have skills that would be useful in the recovery effort, and that would give me full time pay for a while. I was still struggling to make ends meet on part-time pay.

He commented, "Maybe we should let her go – hopefully something will happen so she doesn't come back."

I sat back in the chair and shut my eyes letting tears fall down my cheeks.

"Donna?" my Attorney's voice made me open my eyes. "Are you okay?"

"Ya I guess so," I answered. "It's just hard to realize they hate me so much."

"Don't let it get you down. People do desperate things to protect themselves. And, with that thought, did you know that your conversations were being recorded?"

"What?" I shook my head. "No. When?"

"Every time your Supervisor talked with you, he was taping your conversations." My Attorney replied. "We have the recordings, but while he was good at being sneaky, he was not much good at recording. We can't understand anything on the tapes."

"That's too bad." I said genuinely. "I never said anything I'd be ashamed of, and he did a lot of yelling at me."

At 10 O'clock, my deposition began. The Court Reporter sat at the end of the long conference table. She set up special equipment to record the proceedings.

My Attorney and I sat across the table from the State's Assistant Attorney General who was defending the National Guard and the State. A National Guard JAG (Judge Advocate General) officer sat beside the Defense Attorney.

While the Attorneys chatted easily with each other, I studied the Defense Attorney's face. He reminded me of a weasel. He was thin and had the complexion of a person who spends too much time indoors.

"He's probably a nice man." I thought to myself. "But he's working for the enemy."

The court reporter sound tested her recording equipment, made a few adjustments and we were ready to begin. She asked me if I promised to tell the whole truth and nothing but the truth – I was sworn in and we were ready to begin.

The Defense Attorney asked me questions designed to help him better understand me and what had been done to me.

He was easy to talk to, skilled at drawing people into conversation. While I felt at ease, I kept in mind, "Answer yes or no – don't offer anything he doesn't ask."

After two hours of intense questioning, I was tired. The Defense Attorney smoothly tried to lead me into

106

conversation that would downplay the severity of the crimes committed against me. My brain felt muddled.

My Attorney spoke up, "Excuse me, do we need a break? It's almost noon."

The Defense Attorney said, "Yes, I think that is a good idea. After lunch I have a videotape for us to watch before I begin questioning Ms. Lindahl."

"A videotape?" I thought. "The secret video my Supervisor had made of me?" My heart pounded.

In private conference after lunch my Attorney told me, "I've not seen the video – it is entered into evidence, so we will just have to deal with it." He smiled, "You are doing very well."

The video took well over an hour. It showed me unloading and fueling my mowing equipment, starting my weedeater, and starting my little push mower in the back yard.

The lady who had begged me to mow her yard that day asked my Supervisor, "Why are you recording her?"

"She's defrauding the government." was his reply. She is supposed to be wearing an arm brace."

"I forgot my 'thumb' brace," I thought to myself. "He doesn't realize that I hadn't even seen a doctor for my other elbow."

Watching the video and hearing my Supervisor making damning comments was difficult. It was hard to remain quiet. I clenched my teeth.

As the video showed me doing final touches with my weedeater, blowing grass clippings off the sidewalk and making sure the grass was neatly edged, the lady spoke up, "She does a good job!"

"Yes she does." My Supervisor replied. "And she's like that at the Armory too. She does a good job and she's a hard worker. If she'd just...."

His words faded and couldn't be understood.

"What?" the lady asked.

"She's a hard worker. If she'd just stick to cleaning... and leave the litigating to her lawyers...she'd be a·LOT, better off!"

My jaw wanted to drop, but I maintained a straight face. I felt a sense of excitement from my Attorney.

The videotape clearly depicted intent to harm me.

My deposition continued through the afternoon. I was exhausted by the time the Defense Attorney was done asking questions. Then it was my Attorney's turn to ask me any questions he felt would clarify anything I had said that could be misconstrued.

With my deposition completed, other witnesses were scheduled to be deposed. I was invited to be present as each person was carefully questioned under oath.

For the most part, depositions were what I had expected. People remembered events from their own perspectives. Two depositions stood out.

My female Supervisor appeared nervous and uncertain when she was deposed. She apparently had not remembered what she wrote in her statement to the Air Force Police. The fact that her deposition and her Police Statement conflicted didn't surprise me. She had never been very good at remembering or sometimes understanding facts. I suspected she had a mild learning disability. I didn't want to think that she could be deliberately lying.

She kept insisting that I told her not to do anything about the MSGT's sexual misconduct – she did remember telling me we had to have proof.

But I was astonished to learn that before her retirement, while I was out on medical leave, she had told the Armory Commander about my complaints against the MSGT. She claimed, however, that I had proof but for some obscure reason had destroyed it myself.

She did not recall, either by choice or by mental defect, that when I came to her after being tricked by the MSGT to photograph him nude instead of posing with a flag across his back, he himself had deleted the photos from my camera.

It was shocking to learn that even before I had sought protection from the Air Force Police, the Armory Commander knew what the MSGT had been doing to me.

If the Commander had asked the MSGT about what he was accused of, the MSGT undoubtedly played it down by saying I "wanted him" and "participated" in his sexual misconduct.

The MSGT's statement to the Air Force Police was sickening to read – it was filled with alleged quotes by me saying things like "go, baby go" and "I want it." His police report was so disgusting to me, I burned it. I didn't want such filth in my home.

The pieces were coming together. The former and current Armory Commanders believed the MSGT, their friend, and therefore didn't bother asking me for my side of the story.

My suspension without pay began to make sense. The MSGT had convinced them that I wanted him sexually. But it didn't explain why I had gone to my Supervisor, carefully following the chain-of-command rules, to seek protection.

My Supervisor knew deep down that she was failing to protect me, and before she retired she had, in her words, "gotten it off her chest" by finally moving my complaint up the chain of command.

The other deposition that shocked me was that of the BN (Battalion) Commander. He seemed genuinely surprised to have been deposed and even more surprised to learn I had been suspended without pay.

The BN Commander remembered clearly the Air Force Police turning their investigation of the MSGT over to him. He took immediate action in the military way. He tasked the Armory Commander with investigating the situation in the Armory.

The Armory Commander, failed to conduct a real investigation – complete with interviewing the alleged perpetrator and the victim. Instead he had set into motion my proposed suspension.

The BN Commander had been conveniently removed from my chain-of-command. My response to the proposed suspension went from the Armory Commander to my Human Resources Person – carefully bypassing the BN Commander.

The military way is to give an order and move on, trusting the people under your command to fully take care of the issue.

The BN Commander, in answer to my Attorney's questions, said that sexual harassment and retaliation are despicable and not to be tolerated. He regretted that he had trusted the Armory Commander so completely and he wished he had followed up.

The BN Commander turned from my Attorney, looking directly at me and said that there should have been an investigation to find out the truth. He said that an honest investigation would have proven whether I should have been suspended or if I should have been exonerated for coming forward.

I shut my eyes and squeezed the sudden rush of tears back into my eyes. I had wondered why the BN Commander hadn't done anything to help me. He was a soldier I trusted – he was gung-ho military, all about rules and regulations. Why had he looked the other way – seemingly condoning or covering up the MSGT's sexual misconduct?

I finally understood.

The discovery stage was enlightening. I was hated for accusing a male National Guard Soldier of wrongdoing. Female soldiers knew better than to complain. I as a female civilian had broken the unwritten rule about keeping silence.

I told a female soldier in Delta Company about my legal action against the National Guard for retaliation. She warned me that things go very bad for women who go blow the whistle. She had fought off and eventually endured physical overtures by the Armory Commander. While feeling thoroughly violated, didn't dare take any action. Shrugging her shoulders she justified tolerating abuse, "It's just my body."

Clearly it was more than her body – being sexually assaulted affected her emotions and her mind and her ability to work. But, she knew that complaining would kill her career, and she was a single mom struggling to take care of her children.

Her suffering made my legal action seem even more important. I was determined to pave the way for women to stand up to sexual harassment – report it – protect themselves – take action. I believed that my day in court would help women in the military and perhaps help women everywhere.

The Armory workplace became much more tolerable when the Commander's tour of duty ended and a new Armory Commander took over.

The new Commander returned all my Armory work keys to me and at my request, named the new S-4 Sergeant as my Supervisor.

My New Supervisor was shocked at my personnel file. He called me into his office and asked, "Do you realize how much crap is in your file? With your permission, I'm going to clean it up."

It was easier working without expecting all hell to break loose at any moment, but it was too late to repair the damage already done. I had spent too many years gripping floor equipment too hard and fearing to report that my hands were failing me.

As it turned I didn't have to worry about further damaging my body. My time with the National Guard was over. I received two weeks notification from National Guard Headquarters that my position had been eliminated.

To preserve what remained of my life insurance, I had to cash in my chips and take an early retirement.

I entered the job-search world with several disadvantages, my age, my hands and the feeling that there was a statement next to my name – "don't hire her, she complains."

CHAPTER 13
Trial by Jury

The wheels of justice moved slowly. Seven years after the MSGT began sexually assaulting me, I finally was going to have my day in court.

Because I had not immediately sought legal help, I missed the statute of limitations cut-off date for filing sexual harassment charges. My case dealt only with the charge of retaliation for having gone to the police.

The five day trial was set for the week prior to Easter, 2010. Monday began with jury selection.

I sat with my Attorney at the Plaintiff's table facing the fifty-three people who had been summoned for jury duty. The Attorneys took turns questioning the potential jurors. The goal was to gain jurors who seemed most likely to favor their side.

In a Jury Trial, the Jury decides the case and therefore receive as much respect and honor as the Judge him or herself.

After the eleven jurors and two alternates were chosen and instructed, I was sworn in and my attorney began his direct examination. First I was asked to introduce myself to the courtroom – where I live, my hobbies, my family.

The Defense Attorney objected as I began talking about my children, Andy and Amy. He didn't want the Jury to know that Amy had committed suicide.

The Judge allowed me to tell the Jury that Amy had died at age fourteen and that I was still caring for her horse who was due to foal any day. I described farm chores caring for the animals, baling hay etc. As I spoke about my farm and animals I faced the jury. I wanted them to see me as I was – just a normal person trying to do a good job at work and take good care of my animals at home. I sensed that most of the jurors felt I was genuine.

Answering questions my Attorney asked was not always easy. The Defense Attorney objected frequently, breaking my train of thought.

Describing the sexual harassment and retaliation was particularly difficult. I am a very private person and was raised to not use certain words.

Despite the fact that my Attorney tried to make it easy for me to tell the jury what happened, I was exhausted at the end of the day. Before we were dismissed, the Jury was instructed not to speak to anyone regarding the case – they were not to even talk among themselves.

On Day two my Attorney continued with his direct exam, once again frequently being interrupted by objections. I noticed a couple Jurors roll their eyes when the Defense Attorney jumped up trying to prevent some fact from reaching the ears of the Jury.

When my Attorney said, "I have no further questions at this time, Your Honor." My heart skipped a few beats. It had been difficult enough being questioned by my own Attorney – I braced myself for the worst when the "enemy" took the floor.

I wasn't surprised when the Defense Attorney used tactics designed to trip me into saying things that were not true. He would read a quote, something that I had supposedly said, but he would change key words which also changed the meaning.

For example regarding my thumb he asked, "Does this appear to be a note that you wrote to your Supervisor indicating that your right thumb was *injured?*"

Picking up on the word injured – I answered "Specifically I wrote that it was *aggravated* again – it was a prior problem."

The Defense Attorney was bent on protecting my Supervisor's motives for having secretly videotaped me and for proposing to suspend me – it was a word game. I had to listen carefully as he attempted to put words in my mouth and trick me into changing the facts under oath.

He had no qualms about calling me a liar and accusing me of faking injury and calling me a terrible worker. It hurt me to feel so attacked and put down in front of so many people. It was grueling!

When the Defense Attorney rested, my Attorney asked me a few more questions. He restated the truth and untwisted facts that the Defense Attorney had distorted.

I was glad to be released from the witness chair.

The following days were in many ways even more difficult. As witnesses were questioned, the Defense Attorney misled many of them into outright lies about me. I was shocked that people I had respected would lie under oath.

On the last day of the trial, Good Friday, we were all tired. The Jury listened to the last of the witness examinations and the closing arguments.

I respected my Attorney for his strict adherence to the truth at all times. Yes I had made mistakes and had upset people before I learned that I was expected to follow my chain-of-command. No, I wasn't a perfect employee – there is no perfect employee. But I didn't deserve to be sexually assaulted and then suspended for seeking Police protection when my chain of command failed to protect me.

The Defense Attorney's closing argument was yet another attack on my character and on the quality of my work. It brought me to tears despite myself. I tried to tell myself he was just doing his job, and that he had to say horrible things about me. I just hoped the Jury realized the only defense was to destroy the victim. I felt as though the Defense had won.

The Jury was sent out to deliberate.

I left the courtroom and sat in the hallway pretending to read a book. I wanted to be alone. My old emotional wounds had been poked and prodded and were hurting again.

After a couple hours, my attorney stepped out of the courtroom and said, "The Jury's done."

I watched the courtroom scene in front of me as if in slow motion. Minutes seemed like hours. Did I win? Did I lose?

We stood as the Jurors filed back into their places.

The Judged asked, "Have you reached a verdict?"

"Yes, Your Honor, we have." The Jury Forman replied.

"Bailiff, will you receive the verdict from the foreman and bring it to me?"

The Bailiff carefully carried the piece of paper from the Jury Forman and handed it to the Judge.

The Judge looked at the paper briefly, and then read:

JURY RETURNS AT APPROXIMATELY 4:45 P.M. WITH VERDICT IN THE FOLLOWING FORM: VERDICT A: "ON THE CLAIM OF PLAINTIFF DONNA LINDAHL FOR PERSONAL INJURIES AGAINST DEFENDANTS STATE OF xxxxxxxx AND xxxxxxxxx NATIONAL GUARD, WE, THE UNDERSIGNED JURORS, FIND IN FAVOR OF: PLAINTIFF DONNA LINDAHL. WE, THE UNDERSIGNED JURORS, ASSESS THE DAMAGES OF PLAINTIFF, DONNA LINDAHL, AS FOLLOWS: FOR ACTUAL DAMAGES $0. FOR PUNITIVE DAMAGES $500,000.00"

Stunned – I saw my Attorney smile broadly as he reached to shake my hand. "Congratulations, Donna."

"I won?" My mind could barely take it in. I began crying. Several of the Jurors were sitting in their places crying along with me.

The Judge polled the Jury and accepted their judgment for the record. After the Judge discharged the Jury members they were allowed to speak to me for the first time.

Each Juror shook my hand as they filed past me on their way out of the courtroom. One lady hugged me and through her tears said, "I am so sorry about your daughter and all you've gone through – I just have to hug you."

A male Juror shook my hand firmly, looked me in the eye and said, "Justice has been done this day."

Justice. It was what I had hoped for.

Punitive damages were awarded as punishment, designed to make it clear that sexual harassment and retaliation were not acceptable behaviors, and would not be tolerated.

The hard work, worry and the pain I felt in court was worth it all. I had made a difference! I led the way for women to stand up for their rights in the male military world.

My Attorney's Assistant took me aside and said, "There is a slight problem - the Jury awarded Punitive Damages but for some reason, maybe an oversight, they didn't award Actual Damages."

The Judge called my Attorney and the Defense Attorney to the bench to discuss the problem. In order to award Punitive, there is usually an Actual Damage award, even if only a dollar.

My Attorney wanted to recall the Jury for a decision on Actual Damages, even though it would run the risk of the Jury returning a verdict with no money award. He wanted to be sure we did everything correctly.

The Defense Attorney said that he didn't see a problem with the Jury's not having awarded Actual Damages – he said the Jury had not been told they had to award Actual Damages in order to award Punitive Damages, so they followed the rules and it would be okay.

My Attorney told me not to make plans for the money I had been awarded until he and the Defense Attorney had met with the Judge and I had a check in hand.

No problem - half of my Punitive Damage award would automatically go to a "victim's fund" paying for medical expenses of women who suffered domestic violence.

Money would be very helpful, but most importantly, I had won victory for women.

I was happy. I had been vindicated and I had shown women that we can fight back against sexual harassment.

My joy lasted through Easter weekend - then the battle began all over again.

CHAPTER 14
Appellate Court

Despite his reassuring words about working out the details of the missing Actual Damage award the Defense Attorney never intended to give up the case.

When the Attorneys met with the Judge to finalize paperwork, the Defense Attorney presented a motion to overturn the Jury's verdict.

His motion for "JNOV, Judgment Notwithstanding the Verdict" was based on the case <u>Blue Vs Harrah</u> which set a precedent for needing an award of Actual damages in order to award Punitive damages.

The Judge granted JNOV, overturning the verdict:

COURT TAKES UP PLAINTIFF AND DEFENDANTS PRESENT ARGUMENT. THE COURT, AFTER REVIEWING

ALL MOTIONS, CONDUCTING RESEARCH AND
HEARING ORAL ARGUEMNT, FINDS THAT THE CASE OF
BLUE VS. HARRAH'S CITED IN DEFENDANTS' MOTION
FOR JUDGMENT NOTWITHSTANDING THE VERDICT TO
BE THE CONTROLLING LAW. NO PUNITIVE DAMAGES
CAN BE AWARDED SINCE THERE WAS NO AWARD OF
ACTUAL DAMAGES BY THE JURY. DEFENDANTS'
MOTION FOR JUDGMENT NOTWITHSTANDING THE
VERDICT IS GRANTED. PLAINTIFF'S MOTIONS ARE
DENIED.

My Attorney filed an appeal with the District Court
of Appeals protesting the overturned verdict. The
Appellate Judges reviewed the trial transcript and in
their response in my favor, they quoted directly from the
court record, italicizing words for emphasis:

MY ATTORNEY: "My preference would be to
advise them that they – that this is an inconsistent
verdict, that either there has to be actual and
punitive or none all the way around. I think that
with an instruction they may come back with none
for everything, but I think that that makes more
sense."

DEFENSE ATTORNEY: "*I don't think there is
anything inconsistent about it,* Your Honor. I mean,
they said that there were no actual damages."

THE JUDGE: "How can we – I am just – I am a little stumped myself. I mean, there are not actual damages but there are punitive damages.

MY ATTORNEY: "And there is no instruction that talks about ..."

THE JUDGE: "I have never seen...

MY ATTORNEY: "*to me, that is an inconsistent verdict.*"

DEFENSE ATTORNEY: "The funny thing is that the punitive damages instruction Number 5, does not require them to find actual to get punitive. *I don't know if that is right or not.* You know, that's – I know in federal court that there is a requirement, and it is set out in an instruction."

THE JUDGE: (to the Defense Attorney) "But your opinion is, it just is what it is."

DEFENSE ATTORNEY: "*Yeah. I mean, I think we just have to deal with it.* I think they followed the instructions."

The Appellate Court concluded in part:

Based on the record before this Court, it is clear that the Plaintiff (My Attorney) would have taken the affirmative action of having the jury further instructed on the law to prevent the rendering of this inconsistent verdict *but for the actions of Defendant's counsel.*

Accordingly, were it not for the fact that the defense counsel actively misrepresented to the trial court that the error could be corrected by the trial court after the jury was discharged, it is clear that the Plaintiff would have requested, and the trial court would have instructed, the jury to further deliberate in order to ameliorate the inconsistent verdict.

The Defendant's counsel did not mention the Blue Vs Harrah case to the court (Judge) or the plaintiff's counsel (My Attorney) before the Court dismissed the jury, *nor did he mention that he had represented one of the defendants in the case.*"

Defense counsel, for the first time at oral argument on appeal (when appearing before the Appellate Court) admitted that he was aware of and considering the holding in *Blue* at the time he urged the trial court to accept the jury's inconsistent verdict. He has offered no explanation as to why he would have actively misled the trial court as it pertains to the controlling case precedent in light of the fact that he was one of the primary litigants before this Court in *Blue Vs Harrah*.

Defendant (Defense Attorney) compounded the confusion by representing to the trial court that the parties would just have to deal with the verdict, implying that if there were a problem it could be fixed after the jury was discharged, a scenario that was clearly contrary to the holding in *Blue* which instructs that an inconsistent verdict must be addressed before the jury is discharged.

The Appellate Court further stated that the "Defendant's (Defense Attorney's) "clearly inconsistent" position was at best disingenuous and self serving…"

The Appellate Court Judges' reprimand of the Defense Attorney's sneaky actions made my day!

I was granted a new trial on all counts.

The Defense Attorney appealed to be heard by the State Supreme Court. His request was denied. I wished that the Defense Attorney's appeal to the Supreme case had been successful. The Supreme Court had the power to change laws that would make it safer for women to stand up against sexual harassment.

I was happy, though, to win the right to be heard again in Circuit Court – two years later.

CHAPTER 15
Second Trial

Preparing for trial again was easy in some ways and difficult in others. Depositions had already been taken, the same testimonies would be heard– it was like a rerun. I felt more at ease as I had an idea of what to expect.

Once again the Jury was selected, and the trial moved into the action. The same Judge, bailiff and court reporter ran and recorded the show.

All witnesses swore to tell the truth, the whole truth and nothing but the truth – but this time the Jury did not hear the whole truth.

I was barred from saying anything that may make the Jury sympathize with me. Important facts critical to the case were suppressed. I was barred from saying that I had lost my 14 year old daughter in 1993. I was not allowed to share that my farm is so important to me because of my daughter's horse being left in my care.

In the first trial, the Defense Attorney had tried to put words in my mouth – he would change words and meanings when quoting something I had written or said. During that trial I was allowed to restate what the Defense Attorney claimed I said, and correct his error – this time I was not.

This time when the Defense Attorney presented partial documents and carefully worded twisted facts, I was allowed only yes or no answers. When I tried to explain that he had put documents together out of sequence, thus changing their meaning, he cut me off. I could only answer questions in the exact way they were asked. I couldn't offer any information or correct his intentional misinterpretations.

I swore to tell the "whole truth" but was sternly prevented from letting the Jury hear the truth. The Defense attorney played the manipulation game expertly and I was silenced under threat of mistrial.

After being attacked directly by the Defense Attorney, I was attacked indirectly by the witness for the Defense. I almost expected lightning bolts to shoot from the sky as I listened to Soldiers lie under oath.

An officer I had once held in high regard, perjured himself while wearing his military dress uniform. It was a mockery of God, Truth, and the Army uniform.

It became very clear to me why women don't report sexual harassment. Even when men admit to sexual harassment they go to great lengths to destroy the victim's credibility – and the victim herself.

Sitting in court was painful. It replayed and prolonged the humiliation and frustration of being powerless against ruthless men determined to save their own skin.

The onslaught against me was intense. By the end of the trial, I felt wooden. I felt as though I had succumbed to brainwashing. I shut down my emotions.

After a very brief deliberation the Jury returned a verdict for the Defense. I couldn't blame them – they had heard skillfully distorted facts, partial truths and lies. The focus of the trial shifted from the crimes committed against me to why I deserved to be treated badly.

In my first trial, the Jury saw my mistakes and shortcomings. They saw my blunders through my chain-of-command. Clearly I am not a perfect person or a perfect employee. But the first Jury saw that while I had made mistakes and was imperfect, I had indeed been sexually harassed - and when I sought help from the police, I suffered retaliation. The first Jury voted for Justice.

The second Jury, walking by the limited light they had, rendered a verdict that made it harder for women to consider fighting back against harassment.

I have no doubt that if the first trial were replayed in its entirety for the second Jury, they too would have sent the clear message that sexual harassment and retaliation are not acceptable in today's world – or in today's military society. But they did not hear all the evidence.

If I ever were selected for Jury duty, I would ask if there were pre-trial exclusions in place. Such exclusions make the "whole truth" impossible. Juries should have the right to know all the facts about a trial.

At pre-trial hearings the Attorneys meet with the Judge and decide on ground rules for the trial. For example, the Defense Attorney was not allowed to let his witnesses say outright that they doubted my credibility.

My Attorney was prevented from bringing out the fact that one of my male Supervisors had gotten drunk at a National Guard Convention and had been physically subdued and arrested for sexual harassment. The fact that the Supervisor lost a stripe for his actions was also excluded.

The fact that the Air Force had seized my Supervisor's computer for storing pornography on it was excluded. Also suppressed was the fact that National Guard couldn't pay weekend soldiers for a month because their pay records were stored on the seized computer.

What if the Jury had been given the whole truth - they still may have decided against me – but at least it would have been a complete and honest trial.

I would have rather had all the facts laid out before the Jury – to include my chain-of-command blunders, my naïve belief that the National Guard wanted to follow their own rules, my ambition to move up in State employment, the times I became upset and fought back when treated negatively. Everything should have been laid out for the jury to decide.

I have lost faith in our Justice System. Truth is not as important as the skillful manipulation of facts.

CHAPTER 16
Military Justice

I've often thought, that If my female Supervisor had not been afraid to do the right thing when I reported the MSGT's offensive actions, how different things would be.

If the National Guard had taken seriously their commitment to abide by the Uniform Code of Military Justice and if they had conducted a proper military investigation instead of covering up and protecting one of their high ranking NCO's, I would have been spared – and the military world would be a little safer for female soldiers.

In the civilian world men who are caught "flashing" or exposing themselves to females do jail time. Military Justice is no different. There is a punishment for the crime.

UCMJ Article 134 – Indecent Exposure

1) That the accused exposed a certain part of the accused's body to public view in an indecent manner;

(2) That the exposure was willful and wrongful; and

(3) That, under the circumstances, the accused's conduct was to the prejudice of good order and discipline in the armed forces or was of a nature **to bring discredit upon the armed forces.**

Explanation "Willful" means an intentional exposure to public view. Negligent indecent exposure is not punishable as a violation of the code. *See* paragraph 90c concerning "indecent."

Maximum punishment. Bad-conduct discharge, forfeiture of all pay and allowances, and confinement for 6 months.

The Defense Attorney asked me during my deposition if I thought the MSGT had been punished appropriately – after all he had been relocated and demoted one grade which caused him to lose $700 each month in pay. He eventually retired with honor.

I answered, "I don't feel it was appropriate. The only reason he was relocated was because the Air Force banned him from theAir Base."

"What do you believe would have been appropriate punishment?" he asked.

I replied that I believed if the National Guard had done an honest investigation the MSGT would have been tried in military court.

"And he should have been court-marshaled or discharged?" he asked.

"Yes. He shouldn't have been allowed to retire with honor – he disgraced the military." I answered. "I've listened soldiers being sworn in - soldiers take an oath to defend our country and the constitution against all enemies, foreign and domestic - and to obey orders and abide by the law Military Justice."

The MSGT broke military law. My female Supervisor, out of self-preservation or fear, failed to protect me, a civilian, against what she knew to be violation of military law.

The National Guard's answer to crimes against females within its ranks and within its walls is to look the other way and silence the victim.

I wrote this book because I've been a victim. Unspeakable things have been done to me and to thousands of women in the military. I want crimes against women to be made known - not to gain pity or sympathy – but to inspire outrage!

RESOURCES

*Rape Abuse Incest National Network (RAINN)
24-hour hotline
Phone: 1.800.656.HOPE

*Sexual Assault Resource Agency (SARA)
Phone: 434.977.7273

*Protect Our Defenders - www.protectourdefenders.com

*The Invisible War - www.notinvisible.org

*Sexual Assault Prevention and Response Office (DOD) -
www.sapr.mil

*My Duty to Speak - www.mydutytospeak.com

*Channel 41 News Story
http://www.kshb.com/dpp/news/national/Kansas-City-
woman-declares-war-on-military-sexual-trauma

*

email me at
truly.lindahl@gmail.com